KISS

OF THE

SPIDER WOMAN

AND TWO

OTHER PLAYS

*Also available
in Norton paperback
by Manuel Puig*

TROPICAL NIGHT
FALLING

KISS
OF THE
SPIDER
WOMAN

AND TWO OTHER PLAYS

MANUEL PUIG

W. W. Norton & Company

New York   London

The text of this book is composed in Granjon.
Composition and manufacturing by the Maple-Vail Book Manufacturing Group.
Book design by Beth Tondreau Design.

Library of Congress Cataloging-in-Publication Data

Puig, Manuel.
[Plays. English]
Kiss of the spider woman and two other plays / Manuel Puig :
[translations by Allan Baker and Ronald Christ].
p. cm.
Contents: Kiss of the spider woman—Mystery of the rose bouquet
—Under a mantle of stars.
1. Puig, Manuel—Translations into English. I. Title.
PQ7798.26.U4A2313 1994
862—dc20   ISBN 978-0-393-31148-8   94-6549
ISBN 0-393-31148-1

W. W. Norton & Company, Inc., 500 Fifth Avenue, New York, N.Y. 10110
W. W. Norton & Company Ltd., 10 Coptic Street, London WC1A 1PU

5 6 7 8 9 0

Contents

KISS
OF THE
SPIDER
WOMAN

TRANSLATED BY
ALLAN BAKER

Kiss of the Spider Woman was first presented at the Bush Theatre, London, on 20 September 1985. It was directed by Simon Stokes with the following cast:

MOLINA: Simon Callow
VALENTIN: Mark Rylance

Act One

A small cell in the Villa Devoto prison in Buenos Aires. The stage is in total darkness. Suddenly two overhead white spots light up the heads of the two men. They are sitting down, looking in opposite directions.

MOLINA: You can see there's something special about her, that she's not any ordinary woman. Quite young ... and her face more round than oval, with a little pointy chin like a cat's.

VALENTIN: And her eyes?

MOLINA: Most probably green. She looks up at the

model, the black panther lying down in its cage in the zoo. But she scratches her pencil against the sketch pad, and the panther sees her.

VALENTIN: How come it didn't smell her before?

MOLINA: [deliberately not answering] But who's that behind her? Someone trying to light a cigarette, but the wind blows out the match.

VALENTIN: Who is it?

MOLINA: Hold on. She flusters. He's no matinée idol, but he's nice-looking, in a hat with a low brim. He touches the brim like he's saluting and says the drawing is terrific. She fiddles with the curls of her fringe.

VALENTIN: Go on.

MOLINA: He can tell she's a foreigner by her accent. She tells him that she came to New York when the war broke out. He asks her if she's homesick. And then it's like a cloud passes across her eyes and she tells him she comes from the mountains, some place not far from Transylvania.

VALENTIN: Where Dracula comes from.

MOLINA: The next day he's in his office with some colleagues—he's an architect—and this girl, another architect he works with—and when the clock strikes three he just wants to drop everything and go to the zoo. It's right across the street. And the architect girls asks him why he's so happy. Deep down, she's really in love with him, no use her pretending otherwise.

VALENTIN: Is she a dog?

MOLINA: No, nothing out of this world: chestnut hair, but pleasant enough. But the other one, the one at the zoo, Irene—no, Irina—has disappeared. As time goes by he just can't get her out of his mind until one day he's walking down this fashionable avenue and he notices something in the window of an art gallery. They're pictures by an artist who only paints ... panthers. The guy goes in, and there's Irina being congratulated by all the guests. And I don't remember what comes next.

VALENTIN: Try to remember.

MOLINA: Hold on a sec ... Okay ... then the architect goes up and congratulates her too. She drops the critics and walks off with him. He tells her that he just happened to be passing by, really he was on his way to buy a present.

VALENTIN: For the girl architect.

MOLINA: Now he's wondering if he's got enough money with him to buy two presents. And he stops outside a shop, and she gets a really funny feeling when she sees what kind of a shop it is. There are all different kinds of birds in little cages, sipping fresh water from their bowls.

VALENTIN: Excuse me ... is there any water in the bottle?

MOLINA: Yes, I filled it up when they let us out to the lavatory.

[*The white light which up till now has lit just their heads widens to fully light both actors: we see the cell for the first time.*]

VALENTIN: That's okay then.

MOLINA: Do you want some? It's nice and cool.

VALENTIN: No, or we won't have enough for tea in the morning.

MOLINA: Don't exaggerate. We've got enough to last all day.

VALENTIN: Don't spoil me. I forgot to fetch some when they let us out to shower. If it wasn't for you, we wouldn't have any.

MOLINA: Look, there's plenty ... Anyway, when they go inside that shop it's like—I don't know what—it's like the devil just came in. The birds, blind with fear, hurl themselves against the wire mesh and hurt their wings. She grabs his hand and drags him outside. Straight away the birds calm down. She asks him to let her go home. When he comes back into the shop, the birds are chirruping and singing just like normal and he buys one for the other girl's birthday. And then ... it's no good, I can't remember what happens next, I'm pooped.

VALENTIN: Just a little more.

MOLINA: When I'm sleepy, my memory goes. I'll carry on with the morning tea.

VALENTIN: No, it's better at night. During the day I don't want to bother with this trivia. There are more important things ...

[MOLINA *says nothing.*]

If I'm not reading and I'm keeping quiet, it's because I'm thinking. But don't take it wrong.

[MOLINA *is upset by* VALENTIN'*s remark.*]

MOLINA: [*with almost concealed irony*] I shan't bother you. You can count on that!

VALENTIN: I see you understand. See you in the morning.

[*He settles down to sleep.*]

MOLINA: Till tomorrow. Pleasant dreams of Irina.

[MOLINA *settles down too, but he is troubled by something.*]

VALENTIN: I prefer the architect girl.

MOLINA: I'd already sussed that.

SCENE TWO

*M*OLINA *and* VALENTIN *are sitting in different positions. They do not look at one another. Only their heads are lit; seconds later the night light comes on.*

MOLINA: So they go on seeing each other and they fall in love. She pampers him, cuddles up in his arms, but when he wants to hold her tight and kiss her she slips away from him. She asks him not to kiss her but to let her kiss him with her full lips, but she keeps her mouth shut tight.

[VALENTIN *is about to interrupt, but* MOLINA *forges ahead.*]

So, on their next date they go to this quaint restaurant. He tells her she's prettier than ever in her shimmering black blouse. But she's lost her appetite, she can't manage a thing, and they leave. It's snowing gently. The noise of the city is muffled, but far away you can just hear the growling of wild animals. The zoo's close, that's why. Barely in a whisper she says she's afraid to return to her house and spend the night alone. He hails a taxi, and they go to his house. It's a huge place, all *fin-de-siècle* decor; it used to be his mother's.

VALENTIN: And what does he do?

MOLINA: Nothing. He lights up his pipe and looks over at her. You always guessed he had a kind heart.

VALENTIN: I'd like to ask you something: how do you picture his mother?

MOLINA: So you can make fun of her?

VALENTIN: I swear I won't.

MOLINA: I don't know ... someone really charming. She made her husband happy and her children too. She's always well groomed.

VALENTIN: And do you picture her scrubbing floors?

MOLINA: No, she's always impeccable. The high-necked dress hides the wrinkles round her throat.

VALENTIN: Always impeccable. With servants. People with no other choice than to fetch and carry for her. And, of course, she was happy with her husband who also exploited her in his turn, kept her locked up in the house like a slave, waiting for him . . .

MOLINA: . . . listen . . .

VALENTIN: . . . waiting for him to come home every night from his chambers or his surgery. And she condoned the system, fed all this crap to her son, and now he trips over the panther-woman. Serves him right.

MOLINA: [*irritated*] Why did you have to bring up all that . . . ? I'd forgotten all about this dump while I was telling you the movie.

VALENTIN: I'd forgotten about it too.

MOLINA: Well, then . . . why d'you have to go and break the spell?

VALENTIN: I don't know what you want me to say.

MOLINA: That I have your permission to escape from reality . . . Why should I make myself more depressed than I am already? What's the point in making myself more unhappy . . . ? Otherwise, I'll just go crazy, like Charlotte of Mexico. Though I'd rather be Christina of Sweden, since at least that way I'll end up a queen.

VALENTIN: No, be serious, you're right, being in here can drive you crazy, and not just because it gets you down . . . but because you can alienate yourself just the way you do. This habit of yours, only thinking about the nice things as you call it, that has its own dangers.

MOLINA: That's nonsense . . . How?

VALENTIN: Escaping from reality all the time the way you do becomes a vice, like taking drugs or something. Because, listen to me, reality, *your* reality, isn't only this cell. I mean, if you're reading or studying something, you can transcend whatever cell you're in, do you understand me? That's why I read, that's why I study every day.

MOLINA: Politics ... I don't know what's become of the world, look where it's got us ... you and all those politicians ...

VALENTIN: Stop wingeing like a nineteenth-century housewife ... You're not a housewife, and this isn't the nineteenth century. Tell me a little more of the movie, have we much more to go?

MOLINA: Yes, lots ... Why did I get lumbered with you and not the panther-woman's boyfriend?

VALENTIN: That's another story and one that doesn't interest me.

MOLINA: Frightened to talk about it?

VALENTIN: It bores me. I know all about it—even though you've never said a word.

MOLINA: Fine. I told you I was put away for gross indecency. There's nothing more to add. So don't come the psychologist with me.

VALENTIN: [shielding himself behind humour] Admit that you like him because he smokes a pipe.

MOLINA: No, it's not that, it's because he's gentle and understanding.

VALENTIN: His mother castrated him, that's all.

MOLINA: I like him and that's that. And you like the architect girl—she's not exactly manning the barricades.

VALENTIN: I prefer her to the panther-woman, that's for sure. But the guy with the pipe won't suit you.

MOLINA: Why not?

VALENTIN: Your intentions aren't exactly chaste, are they?

MOLINA: Certainly not.

VALENTIN: Exactly. He likes Irina because she's frigid and he doesn't have to pounce on her, and that's why he takes her to the house where his mother is still present even if she is dead.

MOLINA: [*getting angrier and angrier*] Continue.

VALENTIN: If he's still kept all his mother's things, it's because he wants to remain a child. He doesn't bring home a woman but a child to play with.

MOLINA: That's all in your head. I don't even know if the place is his mother's—I said that because I liked the place, and since I saw antiques in there, I told you it belonged to his mother. For all I know, he rents it furnished.

VALENTIN: So you're making up half the movie?

MOLINA: I'm not, I swear. But—you know—there are some things I add to fill it out for you. The house, for example. And, in any case, don't forget I'm a window-dresser, and that's almost like being an interior designer ... Anyway ... she begins to tell him her story, and I don't remember all the details, but I do remember that in her village, a long time ago, there used to be panther-women. And these tales frightened her a lot when she was a little girl.

VALENTIN: And the birds ... ? Why were they afraid of her?

MOLINA: That's what the architect asks her. And what does she say? She doesn't say anything! And the scene ends with him in pyjamas and a dressing-gown, good quality, no pattern, something serviceable—and he looks at her sleeping on the sofa from his bedroom door, and he lights up his pipe and stands there, all thoughtful.

VALENTIN: Do you know what I like about it? That it's like an allegory of women's fear of submitting to the male, because when it comes to sex, the animal part takes over. You see?

[MOLINA *doesn't approve of* VALENTIN's *comments.*]

MOLINA: Irina wakes up, it's morning already.

VALENTIN: She wakes up because of the cold, like us.

MOLINA: [*irritated*] I knew you were going to say that . . . She wakes up because there's a canary singing in its cage. At first she's afraid to go near it, but the little bird is chirpy so she dares to move a little closer. She heaves a sigh of relief because the bird isn't frightened of her. And then she makes breakfast . . . toast and cereals and pancakes . . .

VALENTIN: Don't mention food.

MOLINA: . . . and pancakes . . .

VALENTINA: I'm serious. Neither food nor women.

MOLINA: She wakes him up and he's all happy to see her settling in, and so he asks her to stay there forever and be his wife. And she says, yes, from the bottom of her heart, and she looks around and the curtains look so beautiful to her, they're made of thick dark velvet. [*aggressively*] And now you can fully appreciate the *fin-de-siècle* decor. Then Irina asks him if he truly wants her to be his wife to give her just a little more time, just long enough for her to get over her fears.

VALENTIN: You can see what's going on with her, can't you?

MOLINA: Hold on. He agrees and they get married. And on their wedding night she sleeps in the bed and he sleeps on the couch.

VALENTIN: Looking at his mother's ornaments. Admit it, it's your ideal home, isn't it?

MOLINA: Of course it is! Now you're going to tell me what they all say.

VALENTIN: What d'you mean? What do they all say?

MOLINA: They're all the same, they all tell me the same thing.

VALENTIN: What?

MOLINA: That I was fussed over as a kid and that's why I'm like I am now, that I was clinging to my mother's skirts, but it's never too late to straighten out, and all I need is a good woman because there's nothing better than a good woman.

VALENTIN: And that's what they all tell you?

MOLINA: And this is what I tell them ... You're dead right ... ! And since there's nothing better than a good woman ... I want to be one! So spare me the advice please, because I know what I feel like, and it's all as clear as day to me.

VALENTIN: I don't see it as clear—at least, not the way you've just put it.

MOLINA: I don't need you telling me what's what—if you want I'll go on with the picture, if not, ciao ... I'll just whisper it to myself, and arrivederci, Sparafucile!

VALENTIN: Who's Sparafucile?

MOLINA: You don't have a clue about opera. He's the hatchet-man in *Rigoletto* ... Where were we?

VALENTIN: The wedding night. He hasn't laid a finger on her.

MOLINA: And I forgot to tell you that they'd agreed she'd go and see a psychoanalyst.

VALENTIN: Excuse me again ... don't get upset.

MOLINA: What is it?

VALENTIN: [*less communicative than ever, sombre*] I can't keep my mind on the story.

MOLINA: Is it boring you?

VALENTIN: No, it's not that. It's ... My head is in a state.
[*He talks more to himself than to* MOLINA.]
I just want to be quiet for a while. I don't know if this has ever happened to you, that you're just about to understand something, you've got the

end of the thread and if you don't yank it now
... you'll lose it.

MOLINA: Why do you like the architect girl?

VALENTIN: It has to come out some way or other ... [*self-contemptuous*] Weakness, I mean ...

MOLINA: Ttt ... it's not weakness.

VALENTIN: [*bitter, impersonally*] Funny how you just can't avoid getting attached to something. It's ... it's as if the mind just oozed sentiment constantly.

MOLINA: Is that what you believe?

VALENTIN: Like a leaky tap. Drips falling over anything.

MOLINA: Anything?

VALENTIN: You can't stop the drips.

MOLINA: And you don't want to be reminded of your girlfriend, is that it?

VALENTIN: [*mistrustful*] How do you know whether I have a girlfriend?

MOLINA: It's only natural.

VALENTIN: I can't help it ... I get attached to anything that reminds me of her. Anyway, I'd do better to get my mind on what I ought to, right?

MOLINA: Yank the thread.

VALENTIN: Exactly.

MOLINA: And if you get it all in a tangle, Missy Valentina, you'll flunk needlework.

VALENTIN: Don't worry on my account.

MOLINA: Okay, I won't say another word.

VALENTIN: And don't call me Valentina. I'm not a woman.

MOLINA: How should I know?

VALENTIN: I'm sorry, Molina, but I don't give demonstrations.

MOLINA: I wasn't asking for one.

SCENE THREE

*N*ight. *The prison light is on.* MOLINA *and* VALENTIN *are sitting on the floor eating.*

VALENTIN: [*speaking as soon as he finishes his last mouthful*] You're a good cook.

MOLINA: Thank you, Valentin.

VALENTIN: It could cause problems later on. I'm getting spoiled.

MOLINA: You're crazy. Live for today!

VALENTIN: I don't believe in that live for today crap. We haven't earned that paradise yet.

MOLINA: Do you believe in heaven and hell?

VALENTIN: Hold on a minute. If we're going to have a discussion, then we need a framework. Otherwise you'll just ramble on.

MOLINA: I'm not going to ramble.

VALENTIN: Okay, I'll state an opening proposition. Let me put it to you like this.

MOLINA: Put it any way you like.

VALENTIN: I can't live just for today. All I do is determined by the ongoing political struggle, d'you get me? Everything that I endure here, which is bad enough ... is nothing if you compare it to torture ... but you don't know what that's like.

MOLINA: I can imagine.

VALENTIN: No, Molina, you can't imagine what it's like ... Well, anyway, I can put up with all this because there's a blueprint. The essential thing is the social revolution, and the pleasures of the senses come second. The greatest pleasure, well, it's knowing that I'm part of the most noble cause ... my ideas, for instance ...

[*The prison lights go out. The blue nighttime light stays on.*]

It's eight . . .

MOLINA: What do you mean, "your ideas"?

VALENTIN: My ideals. Marxism. And that good feeling is one I can experience anywhere, even here in this cell, and even in torture. And that's my strength.

MOLINA: And what about your girlfriend?

VALENTIN: That has to be second too. And I'm second for her. Because she also knows what's most important.

[MOLINA *remains silent.*]

You don't look convinced.

MOLINA: Don't mind me. I'm going to turn in soon.

VALENTIN: You're mad. What about the panther-woman?

MOLINA: Tomorrow.

VALENTIN: What's up?

MOLINA: Look, Valentin, that's me. I get hurt easy. I cooked that food for you, with my supplies, and worse still I give you half my avocado—which is my favorite and could have eaten tomorrow . . . Result? You throw it in my face that I'm spoiling you . . .

VALENTIN: Don't be so soft! It's just like a . . .

MOLINA: Say it!

VALENTIN: Say what?

MOLINA: I know what you were going to say, Valentin.

VALENTIN: Cut it out.

MOLINA: "It's just like a woman." That's what you were going to say.

VALENTIN: Yes.

MOLINA: And what's wrong with being soft like a woman? Why can't a man—or whatever—a dog, or a fairy—why can't he be sensitive if he feels like it?

21

VALENTIN: In excess, it can get in a man's way.

MOLINA: In the way of what? Of torturing someone?

VALENTIN: No, of getting rid of the torturers.

MOLINA: But if all men were like women, then there'd be no torturers.

VALENTIN: And what would you do without men?

MOLINA: You're right. They're brutes, but I need them.

VALENTIN: Molina ... you just said that if all men were like women, there'd be no torturers. You've got a point there; kind of weird, but a point at least.

MOLINA: The way you say things. [*imitating* VALENTIN] "A point at least."

VALENTIN: I'm sorry I upset you.

MOLINA: I'm not upset.

VALENTIN: Well, cheer up then. Don't sulk, man.

MOLINA: Man? What man? Where ...? Tell me so he won't get away ... ! Do you want me to go on with the picture?

VALENTIN: [*trying to hide he finds this funny*] Start.

MOLINA: Irina goes along to the psychoanalyst who's a ladykiller, real handsome.

VALENTIN: Tell me what you mean by real handsome. I'd like to know.

MOLINA: Well, if you're really interested, he isn't my type at all.

VALENTIN: Who's the actor?

MOLINA: I don't remember. Too skinny for my taste. With a pencil moustache. But there's something about him, so full of himself, he just puts you off. And he puts off Irina. She skips the next appointment, she lies to her husband, and instead of going to the doctor's she puts on that black fleecy coat and goes along to the zoo, to look at the panther. The keeper comes along, opens the cage, throws in the meat and closes the door again. But he's absent-minded and leaves the key in the lock. Irina sneaks up to the door and puts her hand on the key. And she just stands there, musing, rapt in her thoughts.

VALENTIN: What does she do then?

MOLINA: That's all for tonight. I'll continue tomorrow.

VALENTIN: At least, let me ask you something.

MOLINA: What?

VALENTIN: Who do you identify with? Irina or the architect girl?

MOLINA: With Irina—who do you think? *Moi*—always with the leading lady.

VALENTIN: Continue.

MOLINA: What about you? I guess you're stuck because the guy is such a wimp.

VALENTIN: Don't laugh—with the psychoanalyst. But I didn't say anything about your choice, so don't mock mine ... You know something? I'm finding it hard to keep my mind on it.

MOLINA: What's the problem?

VALENTIN: Nothing.

MOLINA: Come on, open up a little.

VALENTIN: When you said the girl was there in front of the cage, I imagined it was my girl who was in danger.

MOLINA: I understand.

VALENTIN: I shouldn't be telling you this, Molina. But I guess you've figured it all out for yourself anyhow. My girl is in the organization too.

MOLINA: So what?

VALENTIN: It's only that I don't want to burden you with information it's better you don't know.

MOLINA: With me, it's not a woman, a girlfriend, I mean. It's my mother. She's got blood pressure and a weak heart.

VALENTIN: People can live for years with that.

MOLINA: Sure, but they don't need more aggravation,   23

Valentin. Imagine the shame of having a son inside—and why.

VALENTIN: Look, the worst has already happened, hasn't it?

MOLINA: Yes, but the risk is ever-present inside her. It's that dodgy heart.

VALENTIN: She's waiting for you. Eight years'll fly by, what with remission and all that . . .

MOLINA: [*a little contrived*] Tell me about your girlfriend if you like . . .

VALENTIN: I'd give anything to hold her in my arms right now.

MOLINA It won't be long. You're not in for life.

VALENTIN: Something might happen to her.

MOLINA: Write to her, tell her not to take chances, that you need her.

VALENTIN: Never. Impossible. If you think like that, you'll never change anything in the world.

MOLINA: [*not realizing he's mocking* VALENTIN] And you think you're going to change the world?

VALENTIN: Yes, and I don't care that you laugh. It makes people laugh to hear this, but what I have to do before anything is to change the world.

MOLINA: Sure, but you can't do it all at once, *and* on your own.

VALENTIN: But I'm not on my own—that's it! I'm with her and all those other people who think like we do. That's the end of the thread that slips through my fingers . . . I'm not apart from my comrades—I'm with them, right now . . . ! It doesn't matter whether I can see them or not.

MOLINA: [*with a slight drawl, sceptically*] If that makes you feel good, terrific!

VALENTIN: Christ, what a moron!

MOLINA: Sticks and stones . . .

VALENTIN: Don't provoke me, then. I'm not some loudmouth who just spouts off about politics in a bar. The proof is that I'm in here.

MOLINA: I'm sorry.

VALENTIN: It's okay . . .

MOLINA: [*pretending not to pry*] You were going to tell me something . . . about your girlfriend.

VALENTIN: We'd better drop that.

MOLINA: As you like.

VALENTIN: Why it gets me so upset, I can't fathom.

MOLINA: Better not, then, if it upsets you . . .

VALENTIN: The one thing I shouldn't tell you is her name.

MOLINA: What sort of girl is she?

VALENTIN: She's twenty-four, two years younger than me.

MOLINA: Thirteen years younger than me . . . No, I tell a lie, sixteen.

VALENTIN: She was always politically conscious. First it was . . . well, I needn't be shy with you, at first it was because of the sexual revolution.

MOLINA: [*bracing himself for some saucy tidbit*] I mustn't miss this bit.

VALENTIN: She comes from a bourgeois family, not really wealthy, but comfortably off. But as a kid and all through her adolescence she had to watch her parents destroy each other. Her father cheating her mother, you know what I mean?

MOLINA: No, I don't.

VALENTIN: Cheating her by not telling her he needed other relationships. I don't hold with monogamy.

MOLINA: But it's beautiful when a couple love each other for ever and ever.

VALENTIN: Is that what you'd like?

MOLINA: It's my dream.

VALENTIN: Why do you like men, then?

MOLINA: What's that got to do with it? I want to marry a man—to love and to cherish, for ever and ever.

VALENTIN: So, basically, you're just a bourgeois man?

MOLINA: A bourgeois lady, please.

VALENTIN: If you were a woman, you'd think otherwise.

MOLINA: The only thing I want is to live forever with a wonderful man.

VALENTIN: And that's impossible because ... well, if he's a man, he wants a woman ... you'll always be living in a fool's paradise.

MOLINA: Go on about your girlfriend. I don't want to talk about me.

VALENTIN: She was brought up to be the lady of the house. Piano lessons, French, drawing ... I'll tell you the rest tomorrow, Molina ... I want to think about something I was studying today.

MOLINA: Now you're getting your own back.

VALENTIN: No, silly. I'm tired, too.

MOLINA: I'm not sleepy at all.

SCENE FOUR

---

*N*ight. *The prison lights are on.* VALENTIN *is engrossed in a book.* MOLINA *restless, is flicking through a magazine he already knows backwards.*

VALENTIN: [*lifting his head from the book*] Why are they late with dinner? Next door had it ages ago.

MOLINA: [*ironic*] Is *that* all you're studying tonight? I'm not hungry, thank goodness.

VALENTIN: That's unusual. Don't you feel well?

MOLINA: No, it's just my nerves.

VALENTIN: Listen ... I think they're coming.

MOLINA: Better hide the magazines or else they'll pinch them.

VALENTIN: I'm famished.

MOLINA: Please, Valentin, promise me you won't make a scene with the guards.

VALENTIN: No.

[*Through the grille in the other door come two plates of porridge—one visibly more loaded than the other.* MOLINA *looks at* VALENTIN.]

Porridge.

MOLINA: Yes.

[MOLINA *looks at the two plates which* VALENTIN *has collected from the hatch.*]

[*exchanging an enigmatic glance with the invisible guard*] Thank you.

VALENTIN: [*to the guard*] What about this one? Why's it got less? [*to* MOLINA] I didn't say anything for your sake. Otherwise I'd have thrown it in his face, this bloody glue.

MOLINA: What's the use of complaining?

VALENTIN: One plate's only got half as much as the other. That bastard guard, he's out of his fucking mind.

MOLINA: It's okay, Valentin, I'll take the small portion.

VALENTIN: [*serving* MOLINA *the larger one*] No, you like porridge, you always lap it up.

MOLINA: Skip the chivalry. You have it.

VALENTIN: I told you no.

MOLINA: Why should I have the big one?

VALENTIN: Because I know you like porridge.

MOLINA: But I'm not hungry.

VALENTIN: Eat it, it'll do you good.

[VALENTIN *starts eating from the small plate.*]

MOLINA: No.

VALENTIN: It's not too bad today.

MOLINA: I don't want it.

VALENTIN: Afraid of putting on weight?

MOLINA: No.

VALENTIN: Get stuck in then. This porridge à la glue isn't so bad today. This small plate is plenty for me.

[MOLINA *starts eating.*]

MOLINA: [*overcoming his resistance: his voice nostalgic now*] Thursday. Ladies' day. The cinema in my neighborhood used to show a romantic triple feature on Thursdays. Years ago now.

VALENTIN: Is that where you saw the panther-woman?

MOLINA: No, that was in a smart little cinema in that German neighborhood where all those posh houses with gardens are. My house was near there, but in the run-down part. Every Monday they'd show a German-language feature. Even during the war. They still do.

VALENTIN: Nazi propaganda films.

MOLINA: But the musical numbers were fabulous!

VALENTIN: You're touched.
[*He finishes his dinner.*]
They'll be turning off the lights soon, that's it for studying today. [*unconsciously authoritarian*] You can go on with the film now—Irina's hand was on the key in the lock.

MOLINA: [*picking at his porridge*] She takes the key out of the lock and gives it back to the keeper. The old fellow thanks her, and she goes back home to wait for her husband. She's all out to kiss him, on the mouth this time.

VALENTIN: [*absorbed*] Mmmm . . .

MOLINA: Irina calls him up at his office, it's getting late, and the girl architect answers. Irina slams down the phone. She's eaten up with jealousy. She paces up and down the apartment like a caged beast, and when she walks by the canary she notices it's frenetically flapping its wings. She can't control herself, and she opens the little door and puts her hand right inside the cage. The little bird drops stone dead before she even touches it. Irina panics and flees from the house, looking for her husband, but, of course, she has to go past the bar on the corner and she sees them both inside. And she just wants to tear the other woman to shreds. Irina only wears black clothes, but she's never again worn that blouse he liked so much, the one in the restaurant scene, the one with all the rhinestones.

VALENTIN: What are they?

MOLINA: [*shocked*] Rhinestones! I don't believe this! You don't know ...?

VALENTIN: Not a clue.

MOLINA: They're like diamonds only worthless; little pieces of glass that shine.

[*At this moment the cell light goes out.*]

VALENTIN: I'm going to turn in early tonight. I've had enough of all this drivel.

MOLINA: [*overreacting, but deeply hurt*] Thank goodness there's no light so I don't have to see your face. Don't ever speak another word to me!

[*Note: The production must establish that when the blue light is on—meaning nighttime—* MOLINA *and* VALENTIN *cannot see each other, and so are free to express themselves as they like in gestures and body language.*]

VALENTIN: I'm sorry ...

[MOLINA *stays silent.*]

Really, I'm sorry, I didn't think you'd get so upset.

MOLINA: You upset me because it's one of my favorite movies, you can't know ...

[*He starts to cry.*]

... you didn't see it.

VALENTIN: Are you crazy? It's nothing to cry about.

MOLINA: I'll ... I'll cry if I feel like it.

VALENTIN: Suit yourself ... I'm very sorry.

MOLINA: And don't get the idea you've made me cry. It's

because today's my mother's birthday and I'm dying to be with her ... and not with you. [*Pause.*] Ay ... ! Ay ... ! I don't feel well.

VALENTIN: What's wrong?

MOLINA: Ay ... ! Ay ... !

VALENTIN: What is it? What's the matter?

MOLINA: The girl's fucked!

VALENTIN: Which girl?

MOLINA: Me, dummy. It's my stomach.

VALENTIN: Do you want to throw up?

MOLINA: The pain's lower down. It's in my guts.

VALENTIN: I'll call the guard, okay?

MOLINA: No, it'll pass, Valentin.

VALENTIN: The food didn't do any harm to me.

MOLINA: I bet it's my nerves. I've been on edge all day. I think it's letting up now.

VALENTIN: Try to relax. Relax your arms and legs, let them go loose.

MOLINA: Yes, that's better. I think it's going.

VALENTIN: Do you want to go to sleep?

MOLINA: I don' know ... Ugh! It's awful ...

VALENTIN: Maybe it'd be better if you talk, it'll take your mind off the pain.

MOLINA: You mean the movie?

VALENTIN: Where had we got to?

MOLINA: Afraid I'm going to croak before we get to the end?

VALENTIN: This is for your benefit. We broke off when they were in the bar on the corner.

MOLINA: Okay ... The two of them get up together to leave, and Irina takes cover behind a tree. The architect girl decides to take the shortcut home through the park. He told her everything while they were in the bar, that Irina doesn't make love to him, that she has nightmares about panther-women and all. The other girl, who'd just got used to the idea that she'd lost him, now begins to think maybe she has a chance again. So she's walking along, and then you hear heels clicking behind her. She turns round and sees the silhouette of a woman. And then the clicking gets faster and now, right, the girl begins to get frightened, because you know what it's like when you've been talking about scary things ... But she's right in the middle of the park, and if she starts to run she'll be in even worse trouble ... and, then, suddenly, you can't bear the human footsteps any more ... Ay ... ! Ay ... ! It's still hurting me.

SCENE FIVE

*D*ay. VALENTIN *is lying down, doubled-up with stomach pains.* MOLINA *stands looking on at him.*

VALENTIN: You can't imagine how much it hurts. Like a stabbing pain.

MOLINA: Just what I had two days ago.

VALENTIN: And each time it gets worse, Molina.

MOLINA: You should go to the clinic.

VALENTIN: Don't be thick, I already told you I don't want to go.

MOLINA: They'll only give you a little Seconol. It can't harm you.

VALENTIN: Of course it can; you can get hooked on it. You don't have a clue.

MOLINA: About what?

VALENTIN: Nothing.

MOLINA: Go on, tell me. Don't be like that.

VALENTIN: It happened to one of my comrades once. They got him hooked, his will-power just went. A political prisoner can't afford to end up in prison hospital. You follow me? Never. Once you're in there they come along and interrogate you and you have no resistance ... Ay ... ! Ay ... ! It feels like my guts are splitting open. Aaargh!

MOLINA: I told you not to gobble down your food like that.

VALENTIN: [*raising himself with difficulty*] You were right. I'm ready to burst.

MOLINA: Stretch out a little.

VALENTIN: No, I don't want to sleep, I had nightmares all last night and this morning.

MOLINA: [*relenting, like a middle-class housewife*] I swore I wouldn't tell you another film. I'll probably go to hell for breaking my word.

VALENTIN: Ay ... ! Oh, fucking hell ... !
[MOLINA *hesitates.*]
You carry on. Pay no attention if I groan.

MOLINA: I'll tell you another movie, one for tummyache. Now, you seemed keen on those German movies, am I right?

VALENTIN: In their propaganda machine ... but, listen, go on with the panther-woman. We left off where the architect girl stopped hearing the human footsteps behind her in the park.

MOLINA: Well ... she's shaking with fear, she won't dare turn around in case she sees the panther. She stops for a second to see if she still can't hear the woman's footsteps, but there's nothing, absolute silence, and then suddenly she begins to notice this rustling noise coming from the bushes being stirred by the wind ... or maybe by something else ...
[MOLINA *imitates the actions he describes.*]
And she turns round with a start.

VALENTIN: I think I want to go to the toilet again.

MOLINA: Shall I call them to open up?

VALENTIN: They'll catch on that I'm ill.

MOLINA: They're not going to whip you into hospital for a dose of the runs.

VALENTIN: It'll go away, carry on with the story.

MOLINA: Okay ... [*repeating the same actions*] ... she turns around with a start ...

VALENTIN: Ay ... ! Ay ... ! The pain ...

MOLINA: [*suddenly*] Tell me something: you never told me why your mother doesn't bring you any food.

VALENTIN: She's a difficult woman. That's why I don't talk about her. She could never stand my ideas— she believes she's entitled to everything she's got, her family's got a certain position to keep up.

MOLINA: The family name.

VALENTIN: Only second league, but a name all the same.

MOLINA: Let her know that she can bring you a week's supplies at a time. You're only spiting yourself.

VALENTIN: If I'm in here it's because I brought it on myself, it's got nothing to do with her.

MOLINA: My mother didn't visit lately 'cos she's ill, did I tell you?

VALENTIN: You never mentioned it.

MOLINA: She thinks she's going to recover from one minute to the next. She won't let anyone but her bring me food, so I'm in a pickle.

VALENTIN: If you could get out of this hole, she'd improve, right?

MOLINA: You're a mind-reader ... Okay, let's get on with it. [*repeating the same actions as before*] She turns round with a start.

VALENTIN: Ay ... ! Ay ... ! What have I gone and done? I'm sorry.

MOLINA: No, no ... hold still, don't clean yourself with
the sheet, wait a second.

VALENTIN: No, not your shirt ...

MOLINA: Here, take it, wipe yourself with it. You'll need
the sheet to keep warm.

VALENTIN: No, you haven't got a change of shirt.

MOLINA: Wait ... get up, that way it won't go through
... like this ... mind it doesn't soil the sheet.

VALENTIN: Did it go through?

MOLINA: Your underpants held it in. Here, take them
off ...

VALENTIN: I'm embarrassed ...

MOLINA: Didn't you say you have to be a man ... ? So
what's all this about being embarrassed?

VALENTIN: Wrap my underpants up well, Molina, so they
don't smell.

MOLINA: I know how to handle this. You see ... all
wrapped up in the shirt. It'll be easier to wash
than the sheet. Take the toilet paper.

VALENTIN: No, not yours. You'll have none left.

MOLINA: You never had any. So cut it out.

VALENTIN: Thank you.

[*He takes the tissue and wipes himself and hands
the roll back to* MOLINA.]

MOLINA: You're welcome. Relax a little, you're shaking.

VALENTIN: It's with rage. I could cry ... I'm furious for
letting myself get caught.

MOLINA: Calm down. Pull yourself together.

[VALENTIN *watches* MOLINA *wrap the shirt and
soiled tissue in a newspaper.*]

VALENTIN: Good idea ... so it won't smell, eh?

MOLINA: Clever, isn't it?

VALENTIN: I'm freezing.

[MOLINA *is meanwhile lighting the stove and putting water on to boil.*]

MOLINA: I'm just making some tea. We're down to the

last little bag. It's camomile, good for the nerves.

VALENTIN: No, leave it, it'll go away now.

MOLINA: Don't be silly.

VALENTIN: You're crazy—you're using up all your supplies.

MOLINA: I'll be getting more soon.

VALENTIN: But your mother's sick and can't come.

MOLINA: I'll continue. [*with irony, repeating the same gestures as before but without the same élan*] She turns round with a start. The rustling noise gets nearer, and she lets rip with a desperate scream, when ... whack! The door of the bus opens in front of her. The driver saw her standing there and stopped for her ... The tea's almost ready. [MOLINA *pours the hot water.*]

VALENTIN: Thanks. I mean that sincerely. And I want to apologize ... sometimes I get too rough and hurt people without thinking.

MOLINA: Don't talk nonsense.

VALENTIN: Instead of a film, I want to tell you something real. About me. I lied to you when I told you about my girlfriend. I was talking about another one, someone I loved very much. I didn't tell you the truth about my real girlfriend, you'd like her a lot, she's just a sweet and simple kid, but really courageous.

MOLINA: Please don't tell me anything about her. I don't want to know anything about your political business.

VALENTIN: Don't be dumb. Who's going to question you about me?

MOLINA: They might interrogate me.

VALENTIN: [*finishing his tea; much improved*] You trust me, don't you?

MOLINA: Yes ...

VALENTIN: Well, then ... Inside here it's got to be share and share alike.

MOLINA: It's not that ...

[VALENTIN *lies down on the pillow, relaxing.*]

VALENTIN: There's nothing worse than feeling bad about having hurt someone. And I hurt her, I forced her to join the organization when she wasn't ready for it; she's very ... unsophisticated.

MOLINA: But don't tell me any more now. I'm doing the telling for the moment. Where were we? Where did we stop ... ?

[*Hearing no response,* MOLINA *looks at* VALENTIN, *who has fallen asleep.*]

How did it continue? What comes next?

[MOLINA *feels proud of having helped his fellow cell-mate.*]

SCENE SIX

*D*aylight. *Both* MOLINA *and* VALENTIN *are stretched out on their beds, lost in a private sorrow. In the distance we hear a bolero tune.*

MOLINA *is singing softly.*

MOLINA: "My love, I write to you again
The night brings an urge to inquire
If you, too, dear, recall the tender pain
And the sad dreams our love would inspire."

VALENTIN: What's that you're singing?

MOLINA: A bolero. "My letter."

VALENTIN: Only you would go for that stuff.

MOLINA: What's wrong with it?

VALENTIN: It's romantic eyewash, that's what. You're daft.

MOLINA: I'm sorry. I think I've put my foot in it.

VALENTIN: In what?

MOLINA: Well, after you got that letter, you were really down in the dumps, and here I am singing about sad love letters.

VALENTIN: It was some bad news. You can read it if you like.

MOLINA: Better not.

VALENTIN: Don't start all that again; no one's going to ask you anything. Besides, they read it through before I did.

[*He unfolds the letter and reads it as he talks.*]

MOLINA: The handwriting's like hens' tracks.

VALENTIN: She didn't have much education . . . One of the comrades was killed, and now she's leader of the group. It's all written in code.

MOLINA: Ah . . .

VALENTIN: And she writes that she's having relations with another of the lads, just like I told her.

MOLINA: What relations?

VALENTIN: She was missing me too much. In the organization we take an oath not to get too involved with someone because it can paralyze you when you go into action.

MOLINA: Into action?

VALENTIN: Direct action. Risking your life . . . We can't afford to worry about someone who wants us to go on living because it makes you scared of dying. Well, maybe not scared exactly, but you hate the suffering it'll cause others. And that's why she's having a relationship with another comrade.

MOLINA: You said that your girlfriend wasn't really the one you told me about.

VALENTIN: Damn, staring at this letter has made me dizzy again.

MOLINA: You're still weak.

VALENTIN: I'm shivering and I feel queasy.

[*He covers himself with the sheet.*]

MOLINA: I told you not to start taking food again.

VALENTIN: But I was famished.

[MOLINA *helps* VALENTIN *wrap up well.*]

MOLINA: You were getting better yesterday, and then you went and ate and got sick again. And today it's the same story. Promise me you won't touch a thing tomorrow.

VALENTIN: The girl I told you about, the bourgeois one, she joined the organization with me, but she dropped out and tried to persuade me to split with her.

MOLINA: Why?

VALENTIN: She loved life too much and she was happy just to be with me, that's all she wanted. So we had to break up.

MOLINA: Because you loved each other too much.

VALENTIN: You make it sound like one of your boleros.

MOLINA: Listen, tough guy, haven't you cottoned on yet? Those songs are full of really deep truths, and that's why I like them. The truth is you mock them because they're too close to home. You laugh to keep from crying.... As a tango says.

VALENTIN: I was lying low for a while in that guy's flat, the one they killed. With his wife and kid. I even used to change the kid's nappies ... And do you want to know what the worst of it is? I can't write to a single one of them without blowing them to the police.

MOLINA: Not even your girlfriend?

VALENTIN: [*struggling to hold back his tears*] Oh, God ... ! What a mess ... ! It's all so sad! Give me your hand, Molina. Squeeze hard ...

MOLINA: Hold it tight.

VALENTIN: There's something else. It's wrecking me. It's shameful, awful ...

MOLINA: Tell me, get it off your chest.

VALENTIN: It's ... the girl I want to hear from, the one I want to have next to me right now and hug and kiss ... it's not the one in the movement, but the other one ... Marta, that's her name ...

MOLINA: If that's what you feel deep down ... Oh, I forgot, if your stomach feels real empty, there's a few digestives I'd forgotten all about. [*Without taking his hand from* VALENTIN's *he reaches for the packet of digestives.*]

VALENTIN: For all I shoot my mouth off about progress ... when it comes to women, what I really like is a woman with class, and I'm just like all the reactionary sons-of-bitches that killed my comrade ... The same, exactly the same ...

MOLINA: That's not true ...

VALENTIN: And sometimes I think maybe I don't even love Marta because of who she is but because she's got ... class ... I'm just like all the other class-conscious sons-of-bitches ... in the world.

GUARD'S VOICE: Luis Alberto Molina! To the visiting room! [VALENTIN *and* MOLINA *let go of each other's hand as if caught in a shameful act. The cell door opens and* MOLINA *exits, but not before he's managed to slip the biscuits under* VALENTIN's *blanket. Hereafter, the dialogue is on prerecorded tape. Meanwhile,* VALENTIN *remains onstage and takes the biscuits from under his covers, manages to find just three at the bottom of the large packet and begins to eat them, one at a time, savoring each one.*]

WARDEN'S VOICE: Stop shaking, man, no one's going to do anything to you.

MOLINA'S VOICE: I had a bad stomachache before, sir, but I'm fine now.

WARDEN'S VOICE: You've got nothing to be afraid of. We've made it look like you've had a visitor. The other one won't suspect a thing.

MOLINA'S VOICE: No, he won't suspect anything.

WARDEN'S VOICE: At home last night I had dinner with your benefactor, and he had some good news for you. Your mother is on the road to recovery ... It seems the chance of your pardon is doing her good ...

MOLINA'S VOICE: Are you sure?

WARDEN'S VOICE: What's the matter with you? Why are you trembling ...? You should be jubilant ... Well, have you got any news for me yet? Has he told you anything? Is he opening up to you yet?

MOLINA'S VOICE: No, sir, not so far. You have to take these things a step at a time.

WARDENS VOICE: Didn't it help at all when we weakened him physically?

MOLINA'S VOICE: I had to eat the first plate of fixed food myself.

WARDEN'S VOICE: You shouldn't have done that.

MOLINA'S VOICE: The truth is he doesn't like porridge, and since one portion was bigger than the other ... he insisted I ate it. If I'd refused, he might have got suspicious. You told me, sir, that the doctored food would be on the newest plate, but they made a mistake piling it high like that.

WARDEN'S VOICE: Ah, well, in that case, I'm obliged to you, Molina. I'm sorry about the mistake.

MOLINA'S VOICE: Now you should let him get some of his strength back.

WARDEN'S VOICE: [*irritated*] That's for us to decide. We know what we're doing. And when you get back to your cell, say you had a visit from your mother. That'll explain why you're so excited.

MOLINA'S VOICE: No, I couldn't say that, she always brings me a food parcel.

WARDEN'S VOICE: Okay, we'll send out for some groceries. Think of it as a reward for the trouble with the porridge. Poor Molina!

MOLINA'S VOICE: Thank you, Warden.

WARDEN'S VOICE: Reel off a list of what she usually brings. [*Pause.*] Now!

MOLINA'S VOICE: To you?

WARDEN'S VOICE: Yes, and be quick about it, I've got work to catch up with.

MOLINA'S VOICE: [*as the curtain falls*] Condensed milk, a can of peaches ... two roast chickens ... a big bag of sugar ... two pack of tea, one breakfast, one camomile ... powdered milk, a bar of soap— bathsize—oh, let me think a second, my mind's a complete blank ...

END OF ACT ONE

Act Two

SCENE ONE

*L*ighting as in the previous scene. The cell door opens, and MOLINA
enters with a shopping bag.

MOLINA: Look what I've got!

VALENTIN: No! Your mother's been!

MOLINA: Yes!

VALENTIN: So she's better now?

MOLINA: A little better ... and look what she brought
me. Oops! Sorry, brought us!

VALENTIN: [*secretly flattered*] No, it's for you. Cut the nonsense.

MOLINA: Shut it, you're the invalid. The chickens are for you, they'll get you back on your feet.

VALENTIN: No, I won't let you do this.

MOLINA: It's no sacrifice. I can go without the chicken if it means I don't have to put up with your pong ... No, listen, I'm being serious now, you've got to stop eating this pig-swill they serve in here. At least for a day or two.

VALENTIN: You think so?

MOLINA: And then when you're better ... Close your eyes.
[VALENTIN *closes his eyes, and* MOLINA *places a large tin in one of his hands.*]
Three guesses ...

VALENTIN: Ahem ... er ... er ...
[*Enjoying the game,* MOLINA *places an identical tin in* VALENTIN's *other hand.*]

MOLINA: The weight ought to help you ...

VALENTIN: Heavy all right ... I give up.

MOLINA: Open your eyes.

VALENTIN: Condensed milk!

MOLINA: But you can't have it yet, not until you're better. And this is for both of us.

VALENTIN: Marvelous.

MOLINA: First ... we'll have a cup of camomile tea because my nerves are shot, and you can have a drumstick, no, better not, it's only five ... Anyway, we can have tea and some biscuits, they're even lighter than those digestives.

VALENTIN: Please, can't I have one right away?

MOLINA: Why not! But just with a little marmalade ... !
Luckily, everything she brought is easy to get down so it won't give you any trouble. Except for the condensed milk, for the time being.

VALENTIN: Oh, Molina, I'm wilting with hunger. Why won't you let me have that chicken leg now?

[MOLINA *hesitates a moment.*]

MOLINA: Here ...

VALENTIN: [*wolfing down the chicken*] Honest, I really was beginning to feel bad ...
[*He devours the chicken*]
Thanks ...

MOLINA: You're welcome.

VALENTIN: [*with his mouth full*] But there's just one thing missing to round off the picnic.

MOLINA: Tut, and I thought I was supposed to be the pervert here.

VALENTIN: Stop fooling around! What we need is a movie ...

MOLINA: Ah! Well, never mind ... Now there's a scene where Irina has a completely new hairstyle.

VALENTIN: Oh, I'm sorry, I don't feel too good, it's that dizziness again.

MOLINA: Are you positive?

VALENTIN: Yes, it's been threatening all night.

MOLINA: But it can't be the chicken. Maybe you're imagining it.

VALENTIN: I felt full up all of a sudden.

MOLINA: That's because you wolfed it down without even chewing.

VALENTIN: And this itching is driving me wild. I don't know when I last had a bath.

MOLINA: Don't even think about that. That freezing water in your present state! [*Pause.*] Anyway, she looks stunning here, you can see her reflection in a window pane; it's drizzling and all the drops are running down the glass. She's got raven black hair and it's all scooped up in a bun. Let me describe it to you ...

VALENTIN: It's all scooped up, okay, never mind the silly details ...

MOLINA: Silly, my foot! And she's got a rhinestone flower in her hair.

VALENTIN: [*very agitated now because of his itch*] I know what rhinestones are, so you can save your breath!

MOLINA: My, you are touchy today!

VALENTIN: Can I ask you something?

MOLINA: Go ahead.

VALENTIN: I feel all screwed up—and confused. If it's not too much trouble, I'd like to dictate a letter to her. Would you mind taking it down . . . ? I get dizzy if I try to focus my eyes too hard.

MOLINA: Let me get a pencil.

VALENTIN: You're very kind to me.

MOLINA: We'll do a rough draft first on a bit of paper.

VALENTIN: Here, take my pen-case.

MOLINA: Wait till I sharpen this pencil.

VALENTIN: [*short-tempered*] I told you! Use one of mine!

MOLINA: Okay, don't blow your top!

VALENTIN: I'm sorry, it's just that everything is going black.

MOLINA: Okay, ready, shoot . . .

VALENTIN: [*very sad*] Dear Marta . . . you don't expect this letter . . . In your case, it won't endanger you . . . I'm feeling . . . lonely, I need you, I want to be . . . near you . . . I want you to give me . . . a word of encouragement.

MOLINA: . . . "of encouragement" . . .

VALENTIN: . . . in this moment I couldn't face my comrades, I'd be ashamed of being so weak . . . I have sores all over inside, I need somebody to pour some honey . . . over my wounds . . . And only you could understand . . . because you too were brought up in a nice clean house to enjoy life to the full . . . I can't accept becoming a martyr, it makes me angry to be one ... or, it isn't that, I see it clearer now ... I'm afraid because I'm sick, horribly afraid of dying ... that it may just end here, that my life has amounted to nothing more than this, I never exploited anyone ... and ever since I had any sense, I've been struggling against the exploitation of my fellow man ...

MOLINA: Go on.

VALENTIN: Where was I?

MOLINA: "My fellow man" ...

VALENTIN: ... because I want to go out into the street one day and not die. And sometimes I get this idea that never ever again will I be able to touch a woman, and I can't accept it, and when I think of women I only see you, and what a relief it would be to believe that right until I finish writing this letter you'll be thinking of me ... and that you'll be running your hands over your body I so well remember ...

MOLINA: Hold on, don't go so fast.

VALENTIN: ... over your body I so well remember, and you'll be thinking that it's my hand ... it would be as if I were touching you, darling ... because there's still something of me inside you, isn't that so? Just as your own scent has stayed in my nose ... beneath my fingertips lies a sort of memory of your skin, do you understand me? Although it's not a matter of understanding ... it's a matter of believing, and sometimes I'm convinced that I took something of you with me ... and that I haven't lost it, and then sometimes not, I feel there's just me all alone in this cell ...

[*Pause.*]

MOLINA: Yes ... "all alone in this cell" ... Go on.

VALENTIN: ... because nothing leaves any trace, and my luck in having had such happiness with you, of spending those nights and afternoons and mornings of sheer enjoyment, none of this is any use now, just the opposite, it all turns against me, because I miss you madly, and all I can feel is the torture of my loneliness, and in my nose there is only the stench of this cell, and of myself ... and I can't have a wash because I'm ill, really weak, and the cold water would give me pneumonia, and beneath my fingertips what I feel is the chill of my fear of death, I can feel it in my joints ... what a terrible thing to lose hope, and that's what's happened to me ...

MOLINA: I'm sorry for butting in ...

VALENTIN: What is it?

MOLINA: When you finish dictating the letter, there's something I want to say.

VALENTIN: [*wound up*] What?

MOLINA: Because if you take one of those freezing showers, it'll kill you.

VALENTIN: [*almost hysterical*] And ... ? So what? Tell me, for Christ's sake.

MOLINA: I could help you to get cleaned up. You see, we've got the hot water we were going to use to boil the potatoes and we've got two towels, so we lather one of them and you do your front and I'll do the back and then you can dry yourself with the other towel.

VALENTIN: And then I'd stop itching?

MOLINA: Sure. And we'd clean up a bit at a time so you won't catch cold.

VALENTIN: And you'll help me?

MOLINA: Of course I will.

VALENTIN: When?

MOLINA: Now, if you like. The water's boiling, we can mix it with a little cold water.

[MOLINA *starts to do this.* VALENTIN *can't believe in such happiness.*]

VALENTIN: And I'd be able to get to sleep without scratching?

MOLINA: Take your shirt off. I'll put some more water on.

[*He mixes the hot and cold water.*]

VALENTIN: But you're using up all your paraffin.

MOLINA: I don't mind.

VALENTIN: Give me the letter, Molina.

MOLINA: What for?

VALENTIN: Just hand it over.

MOLINA: Here.

[MOLINA *gives* VALENTIN *the letter.* VALENTIN *starts to tear it up.*]

What are you doing?

VALENTIN: This.

[*He tears the letter into quarters.*]

Let's not mention it again.

MOLINA: As you like . . .

VALENTIN: It's wrong to get carried away like that by despair.

MOLINA: But it's good to get it into the open. You said so yourself.

VALENTIN: But it's bad for me. I have to learn to restrain myself. [*Pause.*] Listen, I mean it, one day I'll thank you properly for all this.

[MOLINA *puts more water on the stove.*]

Are you going to waste all that water?

MOLINA: Yes . . . and don't be daft, there's no need to thank me.

[MOLINA *signals to* VALENTIN *to turn around.*]

VALENTIN: Tell me, how does the movie end? Just the last scene.

MOLINA: [*scrubbing* VALENTIN'*s back*] It's either all or nothing.

VALENTIN: Why?

MOLINA: Because of the details. Her hairdo is very important, it's the style that women wear, or used to wear, when they wanted to show that this was a crucial moment in their lives, because the hair all scooped up in a bun, which left the neck bare, gave the woman's face a certain nobility.

[VALENTIN, *despite the tensions and turmoil of this difficult day, changes his expression and smiles.*]

Why have you got that mocking little grin on your face? I don't see anything to laugh at.

VALENTIN: Because my back doesn't itch any more!

SCENE TWO

*D*ay. MOLINA *is tidying up his belongings with extreme care so as not to wake* VALENTIN. VALENTIN, *nevertheless, wakes up. Both of them are charged with renewed energy, and the dialogue begins at its normal pace but accelerates rapidly into tenseness.*

VALENTIN: Good morning.

MOLINA: Good morning.

VALENTIN: What's the time?

MOLINA: Ten past ten. I call my mother "ten past ten," the poor dear, because of the way her feet stick out when she walks.

VALENTIN: It's late.

MOLINA: When they brought the tea round, you just turned over and carried on sleeping.

49

VALENTIN: What were you saying about your old lady?

MOLINA: Look who's still sleeping. Nothing. Sleep well?

VALENTIN: I feel a lot better.

MOLINA: You don't feel dizzy?

VALENTIN: Lying in bed, no.

MOLINA: Great—why don't you try to walk a little?

VALENTIN: No, you'll laugh.

MOLINA: At what?

VALENTIN: Something that happens to a normal healthy man when he wakes up in the morning with too much energy.

MOLINA: You've got a hard-on? Well, God bless . . .

VALENTIN: But look away, please. I get embarrassed . . .
[*He gets up to wash his face with water from the jug.* MOLINA *puts his hand over his eyes and looks away.*]

MOLINA: My eyes are shut tight.

VALENTIN: It's all thanks to your food. My legs are a bit shaky still, but I don't feel queasy. You can look now.
[*He gets back into bed.*]
I'll lie down a bit more now.

MOLINA: [*overprotective and smothering*] I'll put the water on for tea.

VALENTIN: No, just reheat the crap they brought us this morning.

MOLINA: I threw it out when I went to the loo. You must look after yourself properly if you want to get better.

VALENTIN: It embarrasses me to use up your things. I'm better now.

MOLINA: Button it.

VALENTIN: No, listen . . .

MOLINA: Listen nothing. My mother's bringing stuff again.

VALENTIN: Okay, thanks, but just for today.

[*He collects his books together.*]

MOLINA: And no reading. Rest . . . ! I'll start another film while I'm making the tea.

VALENTIN: I'd better try and study, if I can, now that I'm on form.

[*He starts to read.*]

MOLINA: Won't it be too tiring?

VALENTIN: I'll give it a go.

MOLINA: You're a real fanatic.

VALENTIN: [*throwing the book to the ground as his tenseness increases*] I can't . . . the words are jumping around.

MOLINA: I told you so. Are you feeling dizzy?

VALENTIN: Only when I try to read.

MOLINA: You know what it is? It's probably just a temporary weakness—if you have a ham sandwich you'll be right as rain.

VALENTIN: Do you think so?

MOLINA: Sure, and then later, after you've had lunch and another little snooze, you'll feel up to studying again.

VALENTIN: I feel lazy as hell. I'll just lie down.

MOLINA: [*schoolmistressy*] No, lying in bed only weakens the constitution; you'd be better standing or at least sitting up.

[MOLINA *hands* VALENTIN *his tea.*]

VALENTIN: This is the last day I'm taking any more of this.

MOLINA: [*mistress of the situation*] Ha! Ha! I already told the guard not to bring you any more tea in the morning.

VALENTIN: Listen, you decide what you want for yourself, but I want them to bring me the tea even if it is horse's piss.

MOLINA: You don't know the first thing about a healthy diet.

VALENTIN: [*trying to control himself*] I'm not joking,   51

Molina, I don't like other people controlling my life.

MOLINA: [*counting on his fingers*] Today is Wednesday ... everything will hang on what happens on Monday. That's what my lawyer says. I don't believe in appeals and all that, but if there's someone who can pull a few strings, maybe there's a chance.

VALENTIN: I hope so.

MOLINA: [*with concealed cunning, as he makes more tea*] If they let me out ... who knows who you'll get as a cell-mate?

VALENTIN: Haven't you had breakfast yet?

MOLINA: I didn't want to disturb you. You were sleeping.
[*He takes* VALENTIN's *cup to refill it.*]
Will you join me in another cup?

VALENTIN: No, thanks.
[MOLINA *opens a new packet, not letting* VALENTIN *see.*]

MOLINA: Tell me, what are you going to study later on?

VALENTIN: What are you doing?

MOLINA: A surprise. Tell me what you're reading.

VALENTIN: Nothing ...

MOLINA: Cat got your tongue ... ? And now ... we untie the mystery parcel ... which I had hidden about my person ... and, what have we got here ... ? something that goes a treat with tea ... a cherry madeira!

VALENTIN: No, thanks.

MOLINA: What d'you mean "no" ... ? The kettle's on ... Oh, I know why not—you want to go to the loo. Ask them to open up, and then fly back here.

VALENTIN: For Christ's sake, don't tell me what to do!

[MOLINA *squeezes* VALENTIN's *chin.*]

MOLINA: Oh, come on, let me pamper you a little.

VALENTIN: That's enough ... you prick!

MOLINA: Are you crazy ...? What's the matter with you?

[VALENTIN *hurls the teacup and the cake against the wall.*]

VALENTIN: Shut your fucking trap!

MOLINA: The cake ...

[VALENTIN *is silent.*]

Look what you've done ... If the stove's broke, we're done for ... [*Pause.*] ... and the saucer ... [*Pause.*] ... and the tea ...

VALENTIN: I'm sorry ...

[MOLINA *is silent now.*]

I lost control ... I'm really sorry.

[MOLINA *remains silent.*]

The stove is okay; but the paraffin spilled.

[MOLINA *still doesn't answer.*]

... I'm sorry I got carried away, forgive me ...

MOLINA: [*deeply wounded*] There's nothing to forgive.

VALENTIN: There is. A lot.

MOLINA: Forget it. Nothing happened.

VALENTIN: It did, I'm dying with shame.

[MOLINA *says nothing.*]

... I behaved like an animal ... Look, I'll call the guard and fill up the bottle while I'm at it. We're almost out of water ... Molina, please look at me. Raise your head.

[MOLINA *remains silent.*]

GUARD'S VOICE: Luis Alberto Molina. To the visiting room!

[*The door opens and* MOLINA *exits. The recorded dialogue begins as soon as* MOLINA *moves towards the door.* MOLINA *returns with the provisions to* find VALENTIN *picking up the things he has just thrown on the floor.* MOLINA *starts to unpack the shopping bag. The recorded dialogue is heard while the action takes place onstage.*]

WARDEN'S VOICE: Today's Monday, Molina, what have you got for me?

MOLINA'S VOICE: Nothing, I'm afraid, sir.

WARDEN'S VOICE: Indeed.

MOLINA'S VOICE: But he's taking me more into his confidence.

WARDEN'S VOICE: The problem is they're putting pressure on me, Molina. From the top: from the President's private office. You understand what I'm saying to you, Molina? They want to try interrogation again. Less carrot, more stick.

MOLINA'S VOICE: Not that, sir. It'd be even worse if you lost him in interrogation.

WARDEN'S VOICE: That's what I tell them, but they won't listen.

MOLINA'S VOICE: Just one more week, sir. Please. I have an idea . . .

WARDEN'S VOICE: What?

MOLINA'S VOICE: He's a hard nut, but he has an emotional side.

WARDEN'S VOICE: So?

MOLINA'S VOICE: Well, if the guard were to come and say they're moving me to another block in a week's time because of the appeal, that might really soften him up.

WARDEN'S VOICE: What are you driving at?

MOLINA'S VOICE: Nothing, I swear. It's just a hunch. If he thinks I'm leaving soon, he'll feel like opening up even more with me. Prisoners are like that, sir . . . when one of their pals is leaving, they feel more defenseless than ever.

[*At this moment* MOLINA *is back in the cell, and he takes out the food as the* WARDEN'S VOICE *mentions each item.* VALENTIN *looks at* MOLINA.]

WARDEN'S VOICE: Guard, take this down: two roast chickens, four baked apples, one carton of coleslaw, one pound of bacon, one pound of cooked ham, four French loaves, four pieces of crystalized fruit . . .

[*The recorded voice begins to fade out.*]

. . . a carton of orange juice, two cherry madeiras . . .

[MOLINA *is very calm and sad; he is still upset by* VALENTIN'*s remarks.*]

MOLINA: This is the bacon and this one's the ham. I'm going to make a sandwich while the bread's fresh. You fix yourself whatever you want.

VALENTIN: [*deeply ashamed*] Thank you.

MOLINA: [*reserved and calm*] I'm going to cut this roll in half and spread it with butter and have a sandwich. And a baked apple.

VALENTIN: Sounds delicious.

MOLINA: If you'd like some of the chicken while it's still warm, go ahead. Feel free.

VALENTIN: Thank you, Molina.

MOLINA: We'll each fend for ourselves. Then I won't get on your nerves.

VALENTIN: If that's what you prefer.

MOLINA: There's some crystalized fruit, too. All I ask is that you leave me the pumpkin. Otherwise, take what you want.

VALENTIN: [*finding it hard to apologize*] I'm still embarrassed . . . because of that tantrum.

MOLINA: Don't be silly.

VALENTIN: If I got annoyed with you . . . it was because you were kind to me . . . and I didn't want . . . to treat you the same way.

MOLINA: Look, I've been thinking too, and I remembered something you once said, right . . . ? That when you're involved in a struggle like that, well, it's not too convenient to get fond of

someone. Well, fond is maybe going too far ...
or, why not? Fond as a friend.

VALENTIN: That a very noble way of looking at it.

MOLINA: You see, sometimes I do understand what you
tell me.

VALENTIN: But are we so fettered by the world outside that
we can't act like human beings just for a
minute ... ?

MOLINA: I don't follow.

VALENTIN: Our persecutors are on the outside, not inside
this cell ... The problem is I'm so brainwashed
that it freaks me out when someone is nice to
me without asking anything in return.

MOLINA: I don't know about that ...

VALENTIN: About what?

MOLINA: Don't get me wrong, but if I'm nice to you,
well, it's because I want you to be my friend ...
and why not admit it? I want your affection.
Just like I treat my mother well because she's a
good person and I want her to love me. And
you're a good person too, and unselfish because
you're risking your life for an ideal ... that I
don't understand but, all the same, it's not just
for yourself ... Don't look away like that, are
you embarrassed?

VALENTIN: A bit.

[*He looks* MOLINA *in the face.*]

MOLINA: And that's why I respect you and have warm
feelings toward you ... and why I want you to
like me ... because, you see, my mother's love
is the only good thing I've felt in my life,
because she likes me ... just the way I am.

VALENTIN: [*pointing to the loaf* MOLINA *put aside*] Can I cut
the loaf for you?

MOLINA: Of course ...

VALENTIN: [*cutting the loaf*] And did you never have good friends that meant a lot to you?

MOLINA: My friends were all ... screaming queens, like me, we never really count on each other because ... how can I express it?—because we know we're so easily frightened off. We're always looking, you know, for friendship, or whatever, with somebody more serious, with a man, you see? And that just doesn't happen, right? Because what a man wants is a woman.

VALENTIN: [*taking a slice of ham for* MOLINA'*s sandwich*] And are all homosexuals like that?

MOLINA: Oh no, there are some who fall in love with each other. But me and my friends, we're women. One hundred percent. We don't go in for those little games. We're normal women; *we* only go to bed with men.

VALENTIN: [*too absorbed to see the funny side of this*] Butter?

MOLINA: Yes, thanks. There's something I have to tell you.

VALENTIN: Of course, the movie ...

MOLINA: [*with cunning, but nervous all the same*] My lawyer said things were looking up.

VALENTIN: What a creep I am! I didn't ask you.

MOLINA: And when there's an appeal pending, the prisoner gets moved to another block in the prison. They'll probably shift me within a week or so.

VALENTIN: [*upset by this but dissimulating*] That's terrific ... You ought to be pleased.

MOLINA: I don't want to dwell on it too much, build my hopes ... Have some coleslaw.

VALENTIN: Should I?

MOLINA: It's very good.

VALENTIN: Your news made me lose my appetite.

[*He gets up.*]

MOLINA: Pretend I didn't say anything, nothing's settled yet.

VALENTIN: No, it all looks good for you, we should be happy.

MOLINA: Have some salad.

VALENTIN: I don't know what's wrong, but all of a sudden I don't feel too good.

MOLINA: Is your stomach hurting?

VALENTIN: No . . . it's my head. I'm all confused.

MOLINA: About what?

VALENTIN: Let me rest for a while.

[VALENTIN *sits down again, resting his head in his palms. The light changes to indicate a shift to a different time—the two characters stay where they are: there is a special tension, a hypersensitivity in the air.*]

MOLINA: The guy is all muddled up, he doesn't know how to handle this freaky wife of his. She comes in, sees that he's dead serious and goes to the bathroom to put away her shoes, all dirty with mud. He says he went to the doctor's to look for her and found out that she didn't go anymore. Then she breaks into tears and tells him that she's just what she always feared, a madwoman with hallucinations or even worse, a panther-woman. Then he gives in and takes her in his arms, and you were right, she's really just a little girl for him, because when he sees her so defenseless and lost, he feels again he loves her with all his heart and tells her that everything will sort itself out . . .

[MOLINA *sighs deeply.*]

Ahhh . . . !

VALENTIN: What a sigh!

MOLINA: Life is so difficult . . .

VALENTIN: What's the matter?

MOLINA: I don't know, I'm afraid of building up my hopes of getting out of here ... and that I'll get put in some other cell and spend my life there with God knows what sort of creep.

VALENTIN: Don't lose sight of this. Your mother's health is the most precious thing to you, right?

MOLINA: Yes ...

VALENTIN: Think about her recovery. Period!
[MOLINA *laughs involuntarily in his distress.*]

MOLINA: I don't want to think about it.

VALENTIN: What's wrong?

MOLINA: Nothing!

VALENTIN: Don't bury your head in the pillow ... Are you hiding something from me?

MOLINA: It's ...

VALENTIN: It's what ... ? Look, when you get out of here, you're going to be a free man. You can join a political organization if you like.

MOLINA: You're crazy! They won't trust a fag.

VALENTIN: But I can tell you who to speak to ...

MOLINA: [*suddenly forceful, raising his head from the pillow*] Promise me on whatever you hold most dear, never, never, you understand, never tell me anything about your comrades.

VALENTIN: But who would ever think you're seeing them?

MOLINA: They could interrogate me, whatever, but if I know nothing, I say nothing.

VALENTIN: In any case, there are all kinds of groups, of political action; there are even some who just sit and talk. When you get out, things'll be different.

MOLINA: Things *won't* be different. That's the worst of it.

VALENTIN: How many times have I seen you cry? Come on, you annoy me with your snivelling.

59

MOLINA: It's just that I can't take any more ... I've had
nothing but bad luck ... always.
[*The prison light goes out.*]

VALENTIN: Lights out already ...? In the first place, you
must join a group, avoid being alone.

MOLINA: I don't understand any of that ... [*suddenly
grave*] ... and I don't believe in it much either.

VALENTIN: [*tough*] Then like it or lump it.

MOLINA: [*still crying a little*] Let's ... skip it.

VALENTIN: [*conciliatory*] Come on, don't be like that ...
[*He pats* MOLINA *on the back affectionately.*]

MOLINA: I'm asking you ... please don't touch me.

VALENTIN: Can't a friend pat you on the back?

MOLINA: It makes it worse ...

VALENTIN: Why ...? Tell me what's troubling you ...

MOLINA: [*with deep, deep feeling*] I'm so tired, Valentin
... I'm tired of suffering. I hurt all over inside.

VALENTIN: Where does it hurt you?

MOLINA: Inside my chest and my throat ... Why does
sadness always get you there? It's choking me,
like a knot ...

VALENTIN: It's true, that's where people always feel it.
[MOLINA *is quiet.*]
Is it hurting you a lot, this knot?

MOLINA: Yes.

VALENTIN: Is it here?

MOLINA: Yes.

VALENTIN: Want me to stroke it ... here?

MOLINA: Yes.
[*Short pause.*]

VALENTIN: This is relaxing ...

MOLINA: Why relaxing, Valentin?

VALENTIN: Not to think about myself for a while. Thinking about you, that you need me, and I can be
of some use to you.

MOLINA: You're always looking for explanations ...
You're crazy.

VALENTIN: I don't want events to get the better of me. I
want to know why they happen.

MOLINA: Can I touch you?

VALENTIN: Yes ...

MOLINA: I want to touch that mole—the little round one
over your eye.
[MOLINA *touches the mole.*]
You're very kind.

VALENTIN: No, you're the one who's kind.

MOLINA: If you like, you can do what you want with me
... because I want it too ... If it won't disgust
you ...

VALENTIN: Don't say that—let's not say anything.
[VALENTIN *goes under* MOLINA's *top sheet.*]
Shift a bit closer to the wall ... [*Pause.*] You
can't see a thing, it's so dark.

MOLINA: Gently ... [*Pause.*] No, it hurts too much like
that. [*Pause.*] Slowly please ... [*Pause.*] That's it
... [*Pause.*] ... thanks ...

VALENTIN: Thank you, too. Are you feeling better?

MOLINA: Yes. And what about you, Valentin?

VALENTIN: Don't ask me ... I don't know anything anymore ...

MOLINA: Oh ... it's beautiful ...

VALENTIN: Don't say anything ... not for now ...

MOLINA: It's just that I feel ... such strange things ...
Without thinking, I just lifted my hand to my
eye, looking for that mole.

VALENTIN: What mole ... ? I'm the one with the mole,
not you.

MOLINA: I know, but I just lifted up my hand ... to
touch the mole ... I don't have.

VALENTIN: Ssh, try and keep quiet for a while ...   61

MOLINA: And do you know what else I felt, but only for a minute, no longer ... ?

VALENTIN: Tell me, but keep still, like that ...

MOLINA: For just a minute, it felt like I wasn't here ... not in here, nor anywhere else ... [*Pause.*] It felt like I wasn't here, there was just you ... Or that I wasn't me any more. As if I was ... you.

SCENE THREE

*D*ay. MOLINA *and* VALENTIN *are in their beds.*

VALENTIN: Good morning.

[*He is reinvigorated, happy.* MOLINA *is also highly charged.*]

MOLINA: Good morning, Valentin.

VALENTIN: Did you sleep well?

MOLINA: Yes. [*calmly, not insisting*] Would you like tea or coffee?

VALENTIN: Coffee. To wake me up well—and study. Try to get back into the swing of things ... What about you? Is the gloom over? Or not?

MOLINA: Yes it is, but I feel groggy. I can't think ... my mind's blank.

VALENTIN: I don't want to think about anything either, so I'm going to read. That'll keep my mind off things.

MOLINA: Off what? Feeling guilty about what happened?

VALENTIN: I'm more and more convinced that sex is innocence itself.

MOLINA: Can I ask you a favor ... ? Can we not analyze anything, just for today.

VALENTIN: Whatever you like.

MOLINA: I feel ... fine and I don't want anything to rob

me of that feeling. I haven't felt so good since I was a kid. Since my mother bought me some toy.

VALENTIN: Do you remember what toy you liked most?

MOLINA: A doll.

VALENTIN: Ay!

[*He starts to laugh.*]

MOLINA: What's funny about that?

VALENTIN: As a psychologist I would starve.

MOLINA: Why?

VALENTIN: Nothing ... I was just wondering if there was any link between your favorite toy and ... me.

MOLINA: [*playing along*] It was your own fault for asking.

VALENTIN: Are you sure it wasn't a boy doll?

MOLINA: Absolutely. She had blonde braids and a little Tyrolese folk dress.

[*They laugh together, unselfconsciously.*]

VALENTIN: One question ... Physically, you're as much a man as I am.

MOLINA: Ummm ...

VALENTIN: Why then don't you behave like a man ...? I don't mean with women if you're not attracted to them, but with another man?

MOLINA: It's not me. I only enjoy myself like that.

VALENTIN: Well, if you like being a woman ... you shouldn't feel diminished because of that.

[MOLINA *doesn't answer.*]

I mean you shouldn't feel you owe anyone, or feel obliged to them because that's what you happen to feel like ... You shouldn't yield ...

MOLINA: But if a man is ... my husband, he has to be boss to feel good. That's only natural.

VALENTIN: No, the man and the woman should be equal partners inside the home. Otherwise, it's exploitation. Don't you see?

MOLINA: But there's no thrill like that.

VALENTIN: What?

MOLINA: Since you want to know about it ... the thrill is that when a man embraces you, you're a little bit afraid.

VALENTIN: Who put that idea into your head? That's all crap.

MOLINA: But it's what I feel.

VALENTIN: No, it's not what you feel, it's what you've been taught to feel. Being a woman doesn't make you ... how shall I say ... ? A martyr. And if I didn't think it would hurt like hell, I'd ask you to do it to me, to show you that all this business about being macho doesn't give anyone rights over another person.

MOLINA: [*now disturbed*] This is getting us nowhere.

VALENTIN: On the contrary, I want to talk about it.

MOLINA: Well, I don't, so that's it. I'm begging you, no more, please.

VALENTIN: As you like.

MOLINA: There is something I want to tell you, though ... When you were here it was like I wasn't myself, it was such a relief. And then later, when you were back in your bed ... I still wasn't me, it's so strange, I can't explain.

VALENTIN: Tell me ... try ...

MOLINA: Don't rush me, I have to concentrate ... Yes ... when I was alone in my bed, and I was no longer you, I still felt like I was somebody else, neither male nor female ... what I felt was ...

VALENTIN: ... out of danger ...

MOLINA: Yes! That's it, exactly. How did you know?

VALENTIN: Because it's just what I felt too.

MOLINA: Valentin, why should we feel like that?

VALENTIN: I don't know ...

MOLINA: Valentin ...

VALENTIN: Mmm ...

MOLINA: I'm going to tell you something, but promise me you won't laugh.

VALENTIN: Tell me.

MOLINA: When you come to my bed, afterwards ... I hope I'll never wake up anymore once I've fallen asleep. I'd be sorry for my mother, sure, because she'd be on her own ... but if it was just me, then I wouldn't want to wake ever again. And this isn't just some half-baked notion that I've just dreamed up either, no, it's the honest truth ...

VALENTIN: But first you have to finish the movie.

GUARD'S VOICE: Prisoner Luis Alberto Molina! To the visiting room!

WARDEN'S VOICE: Put me through to your boss, please ... How's it going? Nothing this end. Yes, that's why I called. He's on his way here now ... Yes, they need the information, I'm aware of that ... and if Molina still hasn't found out anything, what should I do with him ... ? Are you sure ... ? Let him out ... But why ... ? Yes, of course, there's no time to lose. Quite, and if the other one gives him a message, Molina will lead us straight to the group ... I've got it, yes, we'll give him just enough time for the other to pass on the message ... The tricky thing will be if Molina catches on that he's under surveillance ... It's hard to anticipate the reactions of someone like Molina: a pervert after all.

[*The cell door opens and* MOLINA *comes back in totally deflated.*]

MOLINA: Poor Valentin, you're looking at my hands.

VALENTIN: I didn't mean to.

MOLINA: Your eyes gave you away, poor love ...

VALENTIN: Such language ...

MOLINA: I didn't get a parcel. You'll have to forgive me ... Ay! Valentin ...

VALENTIN: What's wrong.

MOLINA: Ay, you can't imagine ...

VALENTIN: What's up. Tell me.

MOLINA: I'm going.

VALENTIN: To another cell ...

MOLINA: No, they're releasing me.

VALENTIN: No.

MOLINA: I'm out on parole.

VALENTIN: [*exploding with unexpected happiness*] But that's incredible!

[MOLINA *is confused by the way* VALENTIN *is taking this.*]

MOLINA: You're very kind to be so pleased for me.

VALENTIN: I'm happy for you too, of course ... but, it's terrific! And I guarantee there's not the slightest risk.

MOLINA: What are you saying?

VALENTIN: Listen ... I had to get urgent information out to my people, and I was dying with frustration because I couldn't do anything about it. I was racking my brains trying to find a way ... And you come and serve it to me on a plate.

MOLINA: [*as if he'd just had an electric shock*] I can't do that, you're out of your head.

VALENTIN: You'll memorize it in a minute. That's how easy it is. All you have to do is tell them that Number Three Command has been knocked out and they have to go to Corrientes for new orders.

MOLINA: No, I'm on parole, they can lock me up again for anything.

VALENTIN: I give you my word there's no risk.

MOLINA: I'm pleading with you. I don't want to hear

another word. Not who they are or where they are. Nothing.

VALENTIN: Don't you want me to get out one day too?

MOLINA: Of here?

VALENTIN: Yes, to be free.

MOLINA: There's nothing I want more. But listen to me, I'm telling you this for your own good ... I'm not good at this sort of thing, if they catch me, I'll spill everything.

VALENTIN: I'll answer for my comrades. You just have to wait a few days and then call from a public telephone, and make an appointment with someone in some bogus place.

MOLINA: What do you mean "a bogus place"?

VALENTIN: You just give them a name in code, let's say the Ritz cinema, and that means a certain bench in a particular square.

MOLINA: I'm frightened.

VALENTIN: You won't be when I explain the procedure to you.

MOLINA: But if the phone's tapped, I'll get in trouble.

VALENTIN: Not from a public call-box and if you disguise your voice. It's the easiest thing in the world, I'll show you how to do it. There are millions of ways—a sweet in your mouth, or a toothpick under your tongue ...

MOLINA: No.

VALENTIN: We'll discuss it later.

MOLINA: No!

VALENTIN: Whatever you say.

[MOLINA *flops on the bed, all done in, and buries his face in the pillow.*]

Look at me please.

MOLINA: [*not looking at* VALENTIN] I made a promise, I don't know who to, maybe God, even though I don't much believe in that.

67

VALENTIN: Yes ...

MOLINA: I swore that I'd sacrifice anything if I could only get out of here and look after my mother. And my wish has come true.

VALENTIN: It was very generous of you to put someone else first.

MOLINA: But where's the justice in it? I always get left with nothing ...

VALENTIN: You have your mother and she needs you. You have to assume that responsibility.

MOLINA: Listen, my mother's already had her life, she's lived, been married, had a child ... She's old now, and her life is almost finished ...

VALENTIN: But she's still alive ...

MOLINA: And so am I ... But when is my life going to begin ... ? When is it my turn for something good to happen? To have something for myself?

VALENTIN: You can start a new life outside ...

MOLINA: All I want is to stay with you ...
[VALENTIN *doesn't say anything.*]
Doesn't that embarrass you?

VALENTIN: No ... er, well, yes ...

MOLINA: Yes what?

VALENTIN: That ... it makes me a little embarrassed ... Molina, try to understand this. Everything in a man's life, which may be short or long, is only temporary. Nothing lasts forever.

MOLINA: Maybe ... but why can't it last a little longer, just that at least ... ? If I can relay the information, will you get out sooner?

VALENTIN: It's a way of helping the cause.

MOLINA: But you won't get out sooner. You just think it'll bring the revolution a bit closer.

VALENTIN: Yes, Molinita ... Don't dwell on it, we'll discuss it later.

MOLINA: There's no time left to discuss.

VALENTIN: Besides, you have to finish the panther movie.

MOLINA: It's a sad ending.

VALENTIN: How?

MOLINA: She's a flawed woman ... [*with his usual irony*] All we flawed women come to a sad ending.

VALENTIN: [*laughing*] And the psychoanalyst? Does he get her in the end?

MOLINA: She gets him! And good! No, it's not so terrible, she just tears him to pieces.

VALENTIN: Does she kill him?

MOLINA: In the movie, yes. In real life, no.

VALENTIN: Tell me.

MOLINA: Let's see. Irina goes from bad to worse, she's insanely jealous of the other girl and tries to kill her. But the other one's lucky like hell, and she gets away. Then one day the husband, who's at his wits' end now, arranges to meet the psychoanalyst at their house while she's out. But things get all muddled up, and when the psychoanalyst arrives, she's there on her own. He tries to take advantage of the situation and throws himself at her and kisses her. And right there she turns into a panther. By the time the husband gets home, the guy's bled to death. Meanwhile, Irina has made it to the zoo, and she sidles up to the panther's cage. She's all alone, in the night. That afternoon she got the key when the keeper left it in the lock. It's like Irina's in another world. The husband is on his way with the cops at top speed. Irina opens the panther's cage, and it pounces on her and mortally wounds her with the first blow. The animal is scared away by the police siren, it dashes out into the street, a car runs over it and kills it.

VALENTIN: I'm going to miss you, Molinita.

MOLINA: The movies, at least.

VALENTIN: At least.

MOLINA: I want to ask you for a going-away present. Something that we never did, although we got up to worse.

VALENTIN: What?

MOLINA: A kiss.

VALENTIN: It's true. We never did.

MOLINA: But right at the end, just as I'm leaving.

VALENTIN: Okay.

MOLINA: I'm curious ... Did the idea of kissing me disgust you?

VALENTIN: Ummm ... Maybe I was afraid you'd turn into a panther.

MOLINA: I'm not the panther-woman.

VALENTIN: I know.

MOLINA: It's not fun to be a panther-woman, no one can kiss you. Or anything else.

VALENTIN: You're the spider woman who traps men in her web.

MOLINA: [*flattered*] How sweet! I like that!

VALENTIN: And now it's your turn to promise me something: that you'll make people respect you, that you won't let anybody take advantage of you ... Promise me you won't let anybody degrade you.

GUARD'S VOICE: Prisoner Luis Alberto Molina, be ready with your belongings!

MOLINA: Valentin ...

VALENTIN: What?

MOLINA: Nothing, it doesn't matter ... [*Pause.*] Valentin ...

VALENTIN: What is it?

MOLINA: Rubbish, skip it.

VALENTIN: Do you want ... ?

MOLINA: What?

VALENTIN: The kiss.

MOLINA: No, it was something else.

VALENTIN: Don't you want your kiss now?

MOLINA: Yes, if it won't disgust you.

VALENTIN: Don't get me mad.

[*He walks over to* MOLINA *and timidly gives him a kiss on the mouth.*]

MOLINA: Thank you.

VALENTIN: Thank you.

[*Long pause.*]

MOLINA: And now give me the number of your comrades.

VALENTIN: If you want.

MOLINA: I'll get the message to them.

VALENTIN: Okay . . . Is that what you wanted to ask?

MOLINA: Yes.

[VALENTIN *kisses* MOLINA *one more time.*]

VALENTIN: You don't know how happy you've made me. It's 323–1025.

[*Bolero music starts playing; it chokes* VALENTIN's *voice as he gives his instructions.* MOLINA *and* VALENTIN *separate slowly.* MOLINA *puts all his belongings into a duffel bag. They are now openly broken-hearted:* MOLINA *can hardly keep his mind on what he's doing.* VALENTIN *looks at him in total helplessness. Their taped voices are heard as all this action takes place onstage.*]

MOLINA'S VOICE: What happened to me, Valentin, when I got out of here?

VALENTIN'S VOICE: The police kept you under constant surveillance, listened in on your phone, everything. The first call you got was from an uncle, your godfather; he told you not to dally with minors again. You told him what he deserved, that he should go to hell, because in jail you'd learned what dignity was. Your friends telephoned and you called each other Greta and Marlene and Marilyn, and the police thought maybe it was a secret code. You got a job as a window dresser, and then finally one day you called my comrades. You took your mother to the movies and bought her some fashion magazines. And one day you went to meet my friends, but the police were shadowing you and they arrested you. My friends opened fire and killed you from their getaway car as you'd asked them to if the police caught you. And that was all ... And what about me, Molina, what happened to me?

MOLINA'S VOICE: They tortured you a lot ... and then your wounds turned septic. A nurse took pity on you and secretly he gave you some morphine, and you had a dream.

VALENTIN'S VOICE: About what?

MOLINA'S VOICE: You dreamed that inside you, in your chest, you were carrying Marta and that you'd never ever be apart from one another. And she asked you if you regretted what happened to me, my death, which she said was your fault.

VALENTIN'S VOICE: And what did I answer her?

MOLINA'S VOICE: You replied that I had died for a noble and selfless ideal. And she said that wasn't true, she said that I had sacrificed myself just so I could die like the heroine in a movie. And you said that only I knew the answer. And you dreamed you were very hungry when you escaped from prison and that you ended up on a savage island, and in the middle of the jungle you met a spider woman who gave you food to eat. And she was so lonely there in the jungle, but you had to carry on with your struggle and go back to join your comrades, and your strength was restored by the food the spider woman gave you.

VALENTIN'S VOICE: And, at the end, did I get away from the police, or did they catch up with me?

MOLINA'S VOICE: No, at the end you left the island, you were glad to be reunited with your comrades in the struggle, because it was a short dream, but a pleasant one . . .

[*The door opens:* MOLINA *and* VALENTIN *embrace one another with infinite sadness.* MOLINA *exits. The door closes behind him.*]

CURTAIN

UNDER
A
MANTLE
OF
STARS

TRANSLATED BY
RONALD CHRIST

Under a Mantle of Stars had its premier at the Ipanema Theatre in Rio de Janeiro on 20 August 1982, under the direction of Ivan de Albuquerque, with the following cast:

MASTER OF THE HOUSE: Rubens Corrêa
MISTRESS OF THE HOUSE: Vanda Lacerda
DAUGHTER: Maria Padilha
LADY VISITOR: Leyla Ribeiro
VISITOR: Edson Celulari

Act One

Setting: a spacious living room in an elegant country house. The decor is post–art nouveau and pre–art deco. The year is 1948. It is afternoon and the sunlight has not yet begun to fade. The masters of the house are found seated in the room. Their age is indeterminate: one might guess them to be in their fifties. They also are elegant, but in a very sober, opaque fashion, almost as if they were visible through a grey veil. It is especially striking that the woman has grey hair. Their clothes correspond to the prevailing stereotype of the rural bourgeoisie. He is reading the newspaper; she is doing needlework. Nothing is realistic, everything stylized, including the characters' speech.

MASTER: [*suddenly dropping the newspaper at his side, annoyed*] I can't even read the paper! It's useless trying to distract myself. I can't get the idea out of my head.

MISTRESS: [*conciliatory, but not especially patient*] I'm sure she's coming back. She'll be here before it gets dark.

MASTER: [*gets up, paces nervously*] If only she were our daughter, then we could try to understand her. By way of our own quirks, I mean.

MISTRESS: We *did* raise her.

MASTER: Tonight, darkness is going to swallow her up.

MISTRESS: And some bright, sunny morning we're going to understand her.

MASTER: But she's got other blood, other shadows in her veins. And you can hardly remember the parents, just the way they were, any more than I can. Over the years, we've changed that last image according to our whims. You have embroidered a fleur-de-lis on his chest, just like one of your tapestries.

MISTRESS: Almost twenty years have gone by, and there is something to what you say. We can't possibly remember them as they were.

MASTER: Him—oh, I certainly remember. I see him brought back to life in certain lunatic things his daughter does.

MISTRESS: But it's unfair—to the girl—associating her with that day in the life of her father, his last day. Weren't you two inseparable friends all through your early life? Was one outburst from that ... insignificant wife enough to destroy your friendship with him?

MASTER: [*disheartened*] I wouldn't want anybody to be in my position.

MISTRESS: Oh, why be so negative? ... With or without problems, the girl is ours now. What would have become of us without her? She has filled our days. Just think if she hadn't been born before the accident. You'd still be in the same rage, still have the same doubts. That imbecile wife's phone call, accusing me of adultery, would still be ringing in your ears.

MASTER: They left the child with somebody or other, got into the car with the top down and drove off. They took the curves too fast. He really was my friend, and he was coming here to rid me of that doubt, to tell me it was all a misunderstanding—or was he coming to take my wife away?

MISTRESS: If he was coming to take me away, he would've taken the curves more carefully. My God! ... how boring, answering the same questions over and over for twenty years! That's why I like listening to serials on the radio.

MASTER: Just like a housemaid.

MISTRESS: Don't speak of the devil. Are you sure you put up the ad in a good spot?

MASTER: Yes, I left it in the agency window, and they promised that today they would send that young girl ...

MISTRESS: [*finishes his sentence*] ... that young girl who will be just as perfect—let's hope!—as they described her to you! [*raises her face, for the first time, from her needlework*] Such a tragic face!

MASTER: Without servants there is no time for tragedy, only a sordid bourgeois drama. Passion burns out while you're washing your own dishes and emptying the ashtrays.

MISTRESS: It's better that way ... tragedies on the radio, with background music by the great masters. [*Her expression clouds over, her ironic tone van-*

ishes.] It's this golden sunlight, at four in the afternoon, that stops us from forgetting. We were right here, waiting.

MASTER: The car crashed, and they died instantly—just a few minutes from our door.

MISTRESS: [*regains her usual self-control*] But they left us with the very best of themselves—the daughter. Who is neither strange nor insane. She is ... simply herself. Incomprehensible, period. Like everyone else.

MASTER: But why disappear like this, for hours and hours? She gets up on her horse, and all the horizon shows, far as the eye can see, is some lonesome tree.

MISTRESS: Does it really bother you so much?

MASTER: It's just that one begins to realize ... [*He does not dare to finish.*]

MISTRESS: [*beginning to share her husband's concern*] What?

MASTER: That she's *so* miserable.

MISTRESS: It's not just the usual ups and downs of a girl her age?

MASTER: But what if someday we find out, and it's too late? If one day she can't stand the suffering any more, and she does something foolish? ... I'm very uneasy about this. [*He goes to the telephone.*]

MISTRESS: What are you doing?

MASTER: [*to the operator*] The psychiatric hospital in town, please.

MISTRESS: But what if she finds out? Don't give them her name!

MASTER: [*into the telephone, uneasily*] Excuse me ... Just for information ... In case of an emergency, just in case somebody might need help ... Here, only a few miles ... but out in the middle of the country ... The name? Whose name?

... No ... The patient? ... No ... I'm not ... I am ... the man of the house ... My name? Why? Yes, the emergency might be ... serious ... No, the name, no ... [*hangs up abruptly*]

MISTRESS: Now they're going to suspect ... They can trace our number through the operator.

MASTER: It doesn't matter.

MISTRESS: Care to tell me what you've gained with that absurd call? [*The doorbell rings.*] Who can that be?

MASTER: The maid, thank the Lord.

MISTRESS: [*She goes to open the front door.*] We're saved.

DAUGHTER: [*the fresh voice of a young girl, full of life, radiant, speaking from outside*] Mama, it's me!

MISTRESS: [*opens the door*] Oh ... it's you!

DAUGHTER: [*Dressed according to the dictates of the 1948 Dior "New Look," she is attractive though somewhat ingenuous.*] Some disappointment, isn't it?

MASTER: [*irritated*] May one know what you've been up to? [*resumes staring at the newspaper, pretending not to be interested in the girl*]

DAUGHTER: [*to the* MISTRESS] I left without my key. I forgot to take it.

MASTER: What were you thinking of?

DAUGHTER: I forgot it, just the way I sometimes forget what I want out of life.

MASTER: [*without lifting his head from the paper*] What is it you want?

MISTRESS: Enough of these profundities! She forgets her little whims, that's all she forgets!

DAUGHTER: No, I really do forget what I want most out of life.

MASTER: [*folds the newspaper, throws his head back, leaning it on the back of the sofa, signaling his deep concern*] This morning I had promised myself to work the whole day. You know perfectly well the enormous job ahead of me: to recall the memories of an entire lifetime.

DAUGHTER: Papa, I'm sorry if I upset you ...

MASTER: Just waking up and not finding you was enough.

DAUGHTER: I had to get out in the open, that's all.

MISTRESS: But I noticed you hadn't taken your purse with the money in it. What did you do for lunch?

DAUGHTER: I grabbed some fruit. There's plenty around. Before I forget, he's not coming tonight ... my fiancé, I mean. He says hello to you both. He called this morning.

MISTRESS: You know I adore him, but tonight, I'd really prefer listening to the latest episode of the serial. [addresses her husband] And you?

MASTER: I don't adore him, and, oddly enough, I too would prefer listening to the serial. [He becomes serious.] And so this is what two women have turned me into: [to the DAUGHTER] an alarmist father [to the MISTRESS] and a radio listener.

MISTRESS: Last night, on account of arguing with your father, I missed the episode.

DAUGHTER: I heard it.

MISTRESS: Tell me what happened, right now.

DAUGHTER: Later ... [to the MASTER] Papa, every single minute of yours is precious. For my sake, please, take advantage of the few remaining hours this afternoon.

MASTER: [with an obvious weakness for the DAUGHTER] Thank you. I'll do what I can. [exits, but exchanges an enigmatic look with the MISTRESS just before leaving]

DAUGHTER: [softly, so her father cannot hear] Something terrible's happened, but you have to promise me you won't say a word to him. [points stage left, where the MASTER exited]

MISTRESS: Of course not ...

DAUGHTER: Antonio's not coming tonight—or ever again. He's going to marry another woman. Just as I predicted, he's deserted me.

MISTRESS: But why?

DAUGHTER: There's only one possible reason: [*breathes in deeply, resentful*] marrying for money. She is very rich. But don't say a word to him [*points again to where the* MASTER *exited*] or he'll make a scene.

MISTRESS: Hadn't you noticed anything?

DAUGHTER: From the very start I had the feeling that something bad was going to happen. The joy he brought me was too great, and on my own I began imagining difficulties. From that point to their coming about was a short step.

MISTRESS: Don't beat around the bush. Tell me the facts.

DAUGHTER: I'm sorry, but if you don't listen to me, you're never going to understand. He gave meaning to my life.

MISTRESS: Oh, surely that's not true. You were a happy girl before him.

DAUGHTER: He arrived at the dance that night with another woman. It was the first time I ever saw him, but I had the definite feeling he was someone I'd found before—and lost. And that's what had always disturbed my life, like the moon churning the tides of the sea.

MISTRESS: [*downplaying the significance of what the* DAUGHTER *has just said*] I was eighteen once, too, with an idle imagination.

DAUGHTER: Suddenly all the other men at the dance seemed dull and empty. I took refuge in the library of that big old house, in the dark. My anguish seemed to subside.

MISTRESS: [*ironically*] Suddenly you heard someone breathing.

DAUGHTER: [*challengingly*] Yes. And his voice. He asked me

something. He asked me to describe what he was like, but without seeing him, in the dark. "Why?" I asked.

MISTRESS: [*even more ironically*] Couldn't he recognize himself?

DAUGHTER: He answered that he was lost, and I should point out what he had to do. I shut my eyes in the darkness, and I saw a lake of clear blue liquid that I'd always wished for . . . to drink? . . . to float on? A brilliant blue, with even brighter trimmings. Or did I see some precious stone? An enormous aquamarine, with me swimming inside it. And then he, the one who was lost, changed the tone of his voice, suddenly seeming pleased, and he told me to follow him, because there was still another, an even better place, and I couldn't imagine it for myself. I had seen the entire world, and it was this precious stone, but he told me I was forgetting something: the landscapes inside me, the mountains dark with hatred, the jungles of suffering, where rays of light, like doubts, filtered in, and once again the lake. Only now it is inside me, and someone else must submerge himself in me to appreciate the freshness of the water.

MISTRESS: [*ironically*] A man showed me visions once, too. But I've forgotten them now.

DAUGHTER: I don't ever want to forget them!

MISTRESS: But time takes over, and puts an end to both the good and the bad memories—as well as the desire to live.

DAUGHTER: You really don't remember what you felt?

MISTRESS: No, I've forgotten everything.

DAUGHTER: Antonio will never come here again, but [*gestures stage left*] nobody here should find out. [*An automobile is heard approaching.*]

MISTRESS: Somebody's coming . . .

DAUGHTER: Who could it be? . . .

MASTER: [*appears at the head of the stairs*] Are you expecting anybody? From the window I saw a convertible driving up.

MISTRESS: Let's hope it's the maid.

MASTER: [*coming down the stairs*] In a convertible? [*He asks for silence with a gesture; the car is heard to stop; two car doors open and close, followed by the sound of the front doorbell.*] I'll get it. [*He opens the door. A very elegant couple stands in the shadow of the doorway. They are dressed in the fashion of 1929, almost in full dress you would say. They are young, in their early thirties; but at the same time, their worldly air makes them seem older, of an indeterminate age.*] Hello. What can I do for you?

VISITOR: [*very self-possessed but cordial and polite*] Excuse the intrusion, sir, but . . .

LADY VISITOR: [*She finishes his sentence.*] . . . we were on our way to a place not far from here, and we ran out of gas.

VISITOR: We really have a little left, but we were afraid of ending up in the middle of the countryside, so we stopped here. Are you the man of the house?

MASTER: [*very surprised at recognizing the* VISITORS *when he steps closer to them*] Yes, I am, and it's no intrusion. We'll send for some gasoline . . .

MISTRESS: [*She reacts as he did, but with control, finishing his sentence.*] . . . as soon as the maid gets here, which can't be very long now. But do come in, please. Don't stand out there.

VISITOR: Thank you, madam.

LADY VISITOR: What an inviting room! But don't I recognize it from somewhere? Could it possibly have appeared as a model in one of those interior decorating magazines?

DAUGHTER: Our visitors are going to a masked ball. But are you going to wear masks?

MISTRESS: My dear, don't question people so.

MASTER: Such beautiful clothes, those of twenty years ago.

VISITOR: Excuse me, but I owe a reply to the young lady. Yes, we're going to wear masks.

DAUGHTER: Who do you want to pass for?

VISITOR: For two terrible jewel thieves.

MISTRESS: Do sit down, please.

MASTER: Have you driven far?

LADY VISITOR: Now it's me who's owed a reply. Where can I have seen this charming decor?

DAUGHTER: It's not original. We copied it out of one of the foreign magazines.

MASTER: But you must be thirsty. Driving always parches the throat.

VISITOR: For me, fresh water from that well I saw when we drove up.

MISTRESS: All right. [to the MASTER] Please, you get the water, and [to the DAUGHTER] you get the teapot ready. [to the VISITORS] Excuse me for a moment, while I get the teacups.

DAUGHTER: [to the VISITORS] Excuse me, please. [exits]

MASTER: Excuse me. [exits]

MISTRESS: [alone with the VISITORS] The two of you . . . how can it be?

VISITOR: Do you know us from somewhere?

LADY VISITOR: Yes, she's recognized us . . . [approaches the MISTRESS, perhaps pretending to recognize her] in spite of our disguise . . .

MISTRESS: On the contrary. Except for those clothes, it might never have entered my mind that it was you.

DAUGHTER: [*appears at the extreme left, downstage*] What kind of tea would you like?

LADY VISITOR: Whichever you prefer. I want to have my tea with you.

MISTRESS: [*to the* DAUGHTER] I'll help you and [*to the* VISITOR] be back in just one minute. [*exits, taking the* DAUGHTER *with her*]

LADY VISITOR: [*alone with her partner*] How stupid to mention the jewels!

VISITOR: [*humorously*] Whoever's going to imagine that two people on their way to a masked ball are hiding such a cargo?

LADY VISITOR: [*very disturbed*] Are you sure no one followed us?

VISITOR: Sure. But the ones I don't trust are these people. Where should we hide . . . the loot?

LADY VISITOR: It's not loot. It belongs to us, and if you don't feel that it's yours, well, that's your problem, and the stuff's mine then. [*Finishing the sentence, she contradictorily hands him a silk bag filled with jewels.*]

VISITOR: [*looks around the room*] Where should I put it?

LADY VISITOR: [*lifting up a cushion from the sofa*] No one will suspect this fluffy cushion. [*He puts the bag under the cushion.*] But don't talk to me about anything fluffy. I'm tired to death.

VISITOR: [*ironically*] Well, you like the house. Maybe you'd like to stay here . . .

LADY VISITOR: Yes, I like it, in spite of these bumpkins.

VISITOR: I could leave you here, if you'd prefer it that way.

LADY VISITOR: If you dare leave me, the bosses will turn against you.

VISITOR: [*defiantly*] I'm not so sure about that.

LADY VISITOR: I only have to say one word.

VISITOR: You wouldn't dare!

87

LADY VISITOR: Just one word from me will destroy you.

VISITOR: They're coming . . .

MASTER: [*enters with a cut-glass goblet and an expensive crystal pitcher on a silver tray*] Fresh water from the well. [looks behind him] The girl's making the tea, she can't hear us . . .

LADY VISITOR: [*ambiguously*] Has our arrival caused you a great bother?

MASTER: [*annoyed*] Let's not talk in circles while she's out of the room . . . [*moves to the* LADY VISITOR *and hugs her like an old, much-loved friend*] The two of you! [*with real emotion*] It just can't be . . . You could be an hallucination . . .

VISITOR: Well, perhaps we are one . . .

MASTER: Seems like not a single day has gone by. She . . . is your daughter.

LADY VISITOR: [*entering into the game*] She doesn't know we're alive, then.

MASTER: She believes you both died in the accident, and we told her that we're her foster parents.

LADY VISITOR: What shall we do? Reveal ourselves?

VISITOR: Not right away. That might cause an emotional shock.

MASTER: Let her react on her own. Maybe she'll recognize you naturally. Blood is thicker than water.

DAUGHTER: [*She suddenly appears with the tea tray, completely preoccupied with it. The* MISTRESS *follows.*] This is a kind of tea that has to steep for a few minutes. I hope you like it. Anyway, it's my favorite, as you requested.

LADY VISITOR: Thank you.

MISTRESS: But, please, won't you sit down?

MASTER: [*very confused*] I'm sorry I didn't offer earlier.

VISITOR: [*going to sit down*] Your cushions look really soft and fluffy.

LADY VISITOR: [*seating herself on the cushion covering the jewels*] They are.

MASTER: [*finally offering the water*] Your water. [*The* DAUGHTER *snatches the goblet and serves him.*]

VISITOR: Really, the idea fascinates me: drinking rain water. It's almost like sharing in the freshness of the countryside.

LADY VISITOR: [*with an air of jealousy to her irony*] And the freshness of youth. While I feel like a ship's figurehead next to these women, so natural, wearing no cosmetics.

DAUGHTER: [*rapturously*] Oh, but we both want to be you. Because you've achieved everything you set out to do. You love this man and he is ... [*caught between her fascination with the* LADY VISITOR's *powerful aura and a feeling of indignation, as yet unclarified*] bound to you, maybe forever. Out of everything in the world, he responded to your call.

MISTRESS: Excuse her, please. She gets carried away.

VISITOR: I find her charming. She dares to say whatever comes into her mind.

MASTER: Which is one form of madness. [*to the* DAUGHTER] That's enough, please!

DAUGHTER: [*to the* LADY VISITOR] I always wanted to be you, just as if you were someone I'd known before. But the problem for me is, there can't be two people just the same. [*pointing to the* LADY VISITOR] When you walked through that door, I knew who the conqueror was ...

LADY VISITOR: [*deeply moved by something still unclear*] As if you'd known me before ... You did say that, didn't you?

DAUGHTER: Yes, as if I had seen you somewhere else. Or as if I'd heard a lot about you. Yes, that's it. And then I would have pictured you exactly as I pleased. Less powerful, maybe. But you appear here, and then there's nothing else for me to do but admit it. The conqueror is ... [*points to the* LADY VISITOR *again*]

LADY VISITOR: [*deeply affected*] I would like to be exactly the way you pictured me ... [*smiling*] less fearsome, less powerful, more lovable, right?

MASTER: A child's foolishness! You're splendid just the way you are.

LADY VISITOR: I feel so weary ... all of a sudden.

MISTRESS: The tea might revive you. You haven't even wet your lips.

LADY VISITOR: Would it be possible ... for me to lie down, just for a little while?

DAUGHTER: Yes, of course. [*looks at the* MASTER] Let's take her up to my room. It's quiet enough there, don't you think?

MASTER: Yes. [*stands up*] Here, lean on my arm.

LADY VISITOR: Thank you. [*to the* VISITOR] Can you do without me for a moment?

VISITOR: Please ...

MASTER: Rest yourself a bit. Just think, a grand ball lies ahead of you, isn't that so?

VISITOR: [*to the* LADY VISITOR] Don't worry about me. [*to the others*] Meanwhile, I'd like to venture out into the garden. I caught a glimpse of a strange, though delicate efflorescence, just at the point of opening up.

MISTRESS: [*to the* DAUGHTER] Take good care of the lady.

DAUGHTER: Don't worry.

MASTER: [*He leads the* LADY VISITOR *and the* DAUGHTER *up the stairs and speaks to his wife with evident irony.*] And you take care of the gentleman.

MISTRESS: For the moment, I propose that we all gather

down here at eight o'clock for a glass of champagne.

MASTER: For the moment, make certain he helps himself
to whatever he wants. [*They go up the stairs.*]

VISITOR: Your husband is very kind.

MISTRESS: Do you really want to go out into the garden?
[*She walks about the room to make sure that no
one can see her from upstairs.*] You've finally
come ... you kept your word.

VISITOR: [*unsure how to react*] They can hear you ...
[*gets up*]

MISTRESS: If you love me as much as I love you, you must
realize that hope never dies. When there's so
much love, there's no resigning yourself to losing the other. Deep down inside, something
kept telling me I'd see you again, even in this
world.

VISITOR: [*stalling*] Is that so? ...

MISTRESS: Is it possible the waiting is over? You can't
imagine. These have been years of taking care
of myself, of exercise, dieting, massages. Everything, so you would find me fit. To wait, always
to wait ... in this world. Now my greatest fear
is that hell might be just that: to wait for you
eternally, without your ever arriving.

VISITOR: [*entering into the game*] Fear neither hell, nor
anything else ... because I am here.

MISTRESS: What helped me through each day was ... your
daughter. I always thought I could catch some
trait of yours in her: her way of laying her head
on the pillow, of rubbing her hands together
when it grew cold.

VISITOR: [*even more ambiguously*] She's a lovely girl. I'm
charmed by her.

MISTRESS: Just today we were talking, and she frightened

91

me: repeating things I'd told her, as if they'd
happened to her. Besides ... they were things
you had said to me. Things you remember,
maybe. Very precise words.

VISITOR: A lot of years have gone by ...

MISTRESS: You spoke them to me, one afternoon. I nestled
in your arms, the sun was beginning to set, just
like this very moment. This time of day always
frightens me, the death of the day. Because it's
not absolutely certain the sun will always rise
again. One day or another, things die. That
afternoon when I was waiting for you ... with
him, waiting for you and for ... that woman,
it was growing dark ... and for me the dawn
never came again. Even now, as I'm looking at
you, everything is still plunged in deepest
darkness ...

VISITOR: But I'm here ...

MISTRESS: I can't convince myself. You're a phantom. My
lips remain frozen ... like my thighs.

VISITOR: I'm no phantom. I'm an ordinary man. In a few
hours you'll be able to see my beard growing.

MISTRESS: If you could recall those words, I'd really
believe that you are here—in the flesh.

VISITOR: It's a long time ago, you'll have to give me some
help. At least give me a hint how to start.

MISTRESS: The start ... from the start I had the feeling
that something bad was going to happen. The
joy you brought me was too great, and on my
own I began imagining difficulties. From that
point to their coming about was a short step.

VISITOR: [*feeling his way, not knowing what to say*] You
should have thought about me, about what ...
I'd suffer.

MISTRESS: You arrived at the dance that night with
another woman. It was the first time I ever saw

you, but I had the definite feeling you were someone I'd found before—and lost.

VISITOR: [*trying to lighten the tone a bit*] But what about the other men at the dance, didn't they prevent you from getting to me?

MISTRESS: I took refuge in the library of that big old house, in the dark.

VISITOR: How could I find you in the dark?

MISTRESS: I heard you breathing.

VISITOR: [*trying to follow her lead*] Of course. I was someone you'd found before—and lost.

MISTRESS: [*fascinated*] Lost! I see you're beginning to recall. Because that's the very first word you uttered in that darkened library: "Lost. I'm lost." And you asked me to describe, without opening my eyes, how you were.

VISITOR: What did you answer me?

MISTRESS: You have to recall. Try hard.

VISITOR: [*not knowing what to say*] I've already recalled one thing.

MISTRESS: Yes, that's right. I'll help you a little more. I answered you, without opening my eyes, that I saw a lake, bright blue. Or was it a precious stone? And then you told me to follow, because there was another place, even better, only I couldn't imagine it by myself.

VISITOR: Go on.

MISTRESS: Let's see . . . what was that other place?

VISITOR: Go on, a little more.

MISTRESS: No. Now it's your turn to go on with the story.

VISITOR: This is *your* story. Maybe I have a different one to tell you.

MISTRESS: No. I don't want to hear anything but our story. I don't want to know about anything that might separate us, only about what unites us.

VISITOR: But what about my feelings? You're not interested in knowing about them? Right now I may be going through a terrible crisis. I may need help. Because ... the truth—for this once—may have escaped your imagination.

MISTRESS: [*playfully*] You're testing me, with fibs. I know you're strong, and there's never any need to worry about you. You're not going to fool me. I remember you just the way you were. Strong.

VISITOR: Just the way I still am ... strong.

MISTRESS: But I want you to repeat the rest, without any help from me ... later. You'll have to tell me what that other place was, where you led me. Now, it's almost night, I want to appear before you ... later, in full regalia ... I'll leave you here for quite a while ... I want to adorn myself ... I want you to see me at my very best ... Because now the waiting is over. Tonight I want to blaze, to consume myself in the flame of pleasure, even if it's only once more in my existence ... I want to feel alive. Like those times I used to fall into your arms, on those afternoons in 1929. They were very long, those afternoons.

VISITOR: Don't take too long ...

MISTRESS: [*ironically*] I'm going to, but you will wait for me. Now it's your turn. [*She disappears up the stairs. The* VISITOR *remains perplexed, but at the same time amused. He stretches out on the sofa, worn out after so much feminine effusiveness, and seems to rest. The* DAUGHTER *comes down the stairs. Seeing him apparently asleep, she approaches on tiptoe, strokes his forehead devotedly. He jumps up, but doesn't succeed in standing, because she has sat down next to him and taken hold of his wrists.*]

DAUGHTER: I've got you at my mercy ...

VISITOR: [*He does not know how to react; he obviously does not know her.*] No doubt about that.

DAUGHTER: What a crazy idea of yours! Showing up in disguise. [*She strokes his chest and stands up.*]

VISITOR: [*taking the opportunity to stand up too*] You . . .

DAUGHTER: I took you by surprise? [*She can no longer restrain her desire to embrace him and throws herself into his arms.*] Antonio! Your call this morning almost cost me my life. But now you're here, and it doesn't matter that you've brought her. What's important is holding you in my arms.

VISITOR: It doesn't matter to you . . . about her?

DAUGHTER: [breaks out of the embrace] I hate her! And I also hate that fake beard. [*tears away his artificial beard*]

VISITOR: My companion is dangerous. She must not find out . . . about us.

DAUGHTER: Then she doesn't know . . . that we were engaged, until only a few hours ago, this very morning?

VISITOR: If she finds out, your life—or mine—will be in danger. We have to pretend you've just met me.

DAUGHTER: The truth is, I don't know you. We never made love. Remember, I'm a modern woman, and this is 1948, not the 1920s of your disguise. I'm emancipated. I smoke. And I drink cocktails. And just because I let you put your hands all over my body doesn't mean you know me either. I'm modern, and I know that we will only know each other on the day our flesh is one.

VISITOR: [aroused] I've put my hands all over your body, but what about yours all over mine?

DAUGHTER: I said I was modern, not libertine.

VISITOR: Touch me.

DAUGHTER: What are you saying?

VISITOR: Touch me.

DAUGHTER: Why? To give you a cheap thrill?

VISITOR: [*He is caught up by his strong desire for the young girl and, at the same time, spurred on by the ambiguity of the situation.*] It's just that I'm lost. I've lost myself. And if your hands find me, they'll know how to lead me where I ought to be.

DAUGHTER: [*deeply fascinated*] Lost?

VISITOR: I beg you to tell me, without opening your eyes, how I am.

DAUGHTER: [*taken in by the* VISITOR's *ruse*] Without opening my eyes, I see only the dark landscapes inside me. I'm searching for a place, which they say is inside me, but I don't find it. Someone else has to submerge himself, in my mind, to appreciate the freshness . . . of the water.

VISITOR: A bright-colored lake.

DAUGHTER: [*gratefully surprised*] How do you know that?

VISITOR: You didn't remember?

DAUGHTER: No . . . As soon as you came through that door, I forgot a lot of things. Whatever was beautiful to me before stopped being beautiful, unless it's linked to you somehow.

VISITOR: Could this be the first time you're seeing me?

DAUGHTER: In a certain way, yes.

VISITOR: I peer down into the lake so I can see myself reflected in those brilliant blue waters. Or is it some precious stone?

DAUGHTER: [*lighting up*] Your voice is changing. Suddenly you seem pleased.

VISITOR: Because, in a few moments, I'm going to know you. [*begins to undress her*] But I still can't see myself reflected in the water, such as I am.

DAUGHTER: Maybe that's because inside me the mountains still lie deep in the darkness of night.

VISITOR: It's because you've hidden yourself away in the library of that big old house, in the dark. We'll get out of there.

DAUGHTER: [*dazed by the coincidence of the images*] Oh! . . . I don't know how to get out of there.

VISITOR: Touch me. That's all it takes.

DAUGHTER: [*after delicately kissing him*] You asked me to describe how you are?

VISITOR: [*now really in need of help*] Yes, tell me please.

DAUGHTER: You are exactly as I had always imagined you—the man of my dreams.

VISITOR: No, I, I myself, how am I? . . . I may be in some danger, under the power of some ruthless person, threatened by some crime syndicate. I need your help.

DAUGHTER: You are exactly the one I desired.

VISITOR: No. The man of your dreams, no. I, I myself, how am I? I need you to tell me, so I can know what to do. I'm not someone invented by you.

DAUGHTER: I don't understand you. There's only one man in this room, right?

VISITOR: Yes.

DAUGHTER: And it's you.

VISITOR: [*now without the strength to establish the reality*] Touch me, then. [*He slips his hand under her skirt, then withdraws it, holding her panties.*] As I touch you.

DAUGHTER: I'm afraid I'll fumble with the stubborn knot in your necktie, or with a tight buttonhole, and destroy the magic of this moment.

VISITOR: [*bares his chest, suddenly and determinedly*] I know my knots and my buttonholes.

DAUGHTER: She's tired, your . . . companion, and she won't

come in. But the masters of this house, my dear foster parents, aren't you afraid they'll suddenly appear?

VISITOR: We two are the only ones here.

DAUGHTER: I'm a virgin. I may cry out in pain and spoil everything.

VISITOR: I'll smother any cries with my hand. See? It's a big hand. [*takes her hand*] My knuckles are twice the size of yours—to make you knuckle under. [*Begins to undress her; she pulls back. He gags her with his hand. The* LADY VISITOR *appears at the head of the stairs, dressed in a lavish Chinese robe. She is horrified by what she sees and disappears, only to reappear a moment later followed by the* MASTER *and* MISTRESS, *the latter dressed in a bathrobe and shower-cap. The* VISITOR *goes on undressing the* DAUGHTER, *who does not resist him. The* MASTERS *are also horrified at seeing what is happening, but come down the stairs in silence, following the* LADY VISITOR.]

MISTRESS: [*On reaching the foot of the stairs, she can no longer control her horror.*] Ahhh!

DAUGHTER: [*The pair stop when they hear the exclamation and discover three others in the room, a few feet away from their partially uncovered bodies.*] Antonio!

VISITOR: Don't move.

MASTER: [*pityingly, always acting on the basis of what, for him, is the delicate mental stability of the* DAUGHTER] Don't get upset ... [*powerfully restraining the* LADY VISITOR *from attacking the couple*] Whenever a maiden is deflowered, the same thing always happens: she imagines that her parents discover her in the act.

DAUGHTER: No, you are seeing ...

MASTER: Nothing of the kind. We are an hallucination. It's your guilty conscience that makes you see visions ... [*He repeats his impressive sign to the* LADY VISITOR, *so that she will join in the farce.*]

LADY VISITOR: [*wickedly*] ... and makes you miss out on the festivities.

MISTRESS: No. How horrible ... [*The* MASTER *silences her by covering her mouth with his hand.*]

LADY VISITOR: Take advantage of this moment, and savor it. Don't be foolish. Leave the sorrow until later. It will come, in ways you know nothing about.

DAUGHTER: [*completely confused*] I shouldn't be foolish?

VISITOR: [*resumes undressing her*] Or talkative either. [*Led by the* MASTER, *the two other women draw back and begin to climb the stairs.*] It's better in silence.

DAUGHTER: [*gives him her full attention again*] Why?

VISITOR: Because after a while words may turn against us, caresses never.

DAUGHTER: In silence ... Oh! ... Ay! [*He covers her mouth again.*]

VISITOR: Yes, in silence ... I don't want you talking to the man of your dreams. He may not be here.

CURTAIN

Act Two

Setting: The same as Act I, but in the dark of night. Only one light is on, at stage left, under the staircase. The MASTER smokes and paces agitatedly, like a moth around a flame. The extreme right of the stage, including the sofa where the couple made love, is in total darkness.

LADY VISITOR: [*She is stretched out on the sofa, and suddenly an unnatural light falls on her. Until now the audience has not seen her. She is still dressed in the Chinese robe from the previous act, and she holds an unlit cigarette in her mouth.*] Do you have a light?

MASTER: [*very surprised*] What! You frightened me.

LADY VISITOR: I've been watching you for quite some time.

MASTER: [*approaching to light her cigarette*] I didn't see you.

LADY VISITOR: There's no one blinder than he who doesn't want to see.

MASTER: It's because I'm very nervous, and very confused.

LADY VISITOR: I'm melancholy, which is worse.

MASTER: No. The worst thing is worrying about a loved one. That girl is all we have in life.

LADY VISITOR: Look, everything's not lost. What we've got to do is act, but quickly. And not let our lives be governed by irresponsible types, no matter how much we love them. To love is one thing; to let yourself be manipulated is another.

MASTER: I don't have the slightest idea of what to do. With things as they are, I'm terrified to take even one step. That little girl's psyche is very fragile. She can be hurt very easily.

LADY VISITOR: Calm down, she is not the . . . the little girl you think. She knows perfectly well what she wants, and she doesn't care who she snatches it from.

MASTER: She's not aware of what she's doing.

LADY VISITOR: She has no scruples, which is something else altogether. What she doesn't know is the kind of louse she's gotten herself mixed up with.

MASTER: If he's a louse, why are you with him?

LADY VISITOR: In this case, the danger lies in not knowing who he is. Once you know that, and treat him accordingly, everything untangles itself perfectly.

MASTER: You say it's necessary to act. But how?

LADY VISITOR: The first step is to realize there's a plot to eliminate us. You and me. Later, there will be a third victim, eventually a fourth, and finally, of course, a single survivor.

MASTER: Why plot against me?

LADY VISITOR: You maintain order, and somebody doesn't find that convenient.

MASTER: But why against you?

LADY VISITOR: No one can love me.

MASTER: What are you saying? You're beautiful!

LADY VISITOR: I have power.

MASTER: What power?

LADY VISITOR: It's beside the point to specify. Power such as money gives you, for example. Everyone envies my power. I could destroy him, whenever I like. He knows it and fears me. That's why he can't love me. Power is a curse.

MASTER: No, being powerless is. When I think that one day I may die, leaving that child defenseless, I'm shattered by torment.

LADY VISITOR: No doubt about it: you are mortal. And worse still, three people want you dead. [*A clock strikes.*]

MASTER: Eight o'clock. They'll be coming down now.

LADY VISITOR: I've got an idea. You have to tell a lie ... [*The* MISTRESS *is heard coming down the stairs; she is elegantly attired.*] Come over here with me. [*She leads him stage right, where there is no light. They talk. Meanwhile, the* MISTRESS *reaches the bottom of the stairs and takes glasses out of the cabinet for the champagne.*]

MASTER: I know what lie I have to tell ...

LADY VISITOR: A lie that smashes all their plans into the ground.

MASTER: I'm going to make them tremble ... to cry with regret.

VISITOR: [*He enters from the garden. He is wearing the false beard and has put his shirt on again, but his sleeves are rolled up and his collar is unbuttoned. He speaks to the* LADY VISITOR *and the* MASTER.] Plotting in the dark?

MISTRESS: Ahh! ... I was asking myself where all of you could be.

VISITOR: I'm always on time. I was invited for a glass of champagne, and here I am.

MASTER: [*to the* VISITOR] Did you see the garden?

VISITOR: An orgy of fragrances! The night is pitch black, and I couldn't make out the colors, but the perfumes seemed stronger every minute. They were seducing me, making themselves indispensable. I'll never be able to forget that garden, I'll always miss that perfume ... go wherever I go, [*looks at the* LADY VISITOR] be with whomever I'll be with ...

LADY VISITOR: A good cold in the head, and it will all vanish ...

MASTER: [*with veiled maliciousness*] I was worried, thinking you might be bored, all alone, with nothing to do, while the lady rested. But *I* had something to do. You see, I'm writing my memoirs.

DAUGHTER: [*coming down the stairs, very well dressed, all in white, luminous, springlike*] But don't you think you're very young to be writing your memoirs?

MISTRESS: We're all here now, so let's make a toast, because I'm thirsty. [*She begins to pour the champagne.*]

DAUGHTER: What are we toasting? It's so important to choose the words precisely.

LADY VISITOR: Precisely?

DAUGHTER: Yes, I feel ... happy, and I'd like everybody to share my feelings. I'd like to find the word that will have this same effect on everybody here.

LADY VISITOR: This effect you're talking about—it lasts about half an hour ... and afterwards, best go to sleep. Because while it seems this happiness is forever, any mishap can break the spell. The spell of the champagne, of course. That's what I'm talking about.

MISTRESS: [*deeply involved*] Better not try to find that word, then.

VISITOR: I'll propose one.

MASTER: Which? I have one to propose as well.

VISITOR: I want to drink a toast to ... Antonio. This young lady is in love with a young man named Antonio, who makes her happy. In turn, the daughter's happiness makes her parents happy, so they open their doors to share it all with the rest of the world—in this case represented by two strangers on their way to a masked ball.

MISTRESS: We'll toast Antonio then ...

LADY VISITOR: If the champagne is well chilled, I have no objection.

MISTRESS: It's chilled.

MASTER: To ... Antonio.

DAUGHTER: To the first and only love of my life.

LADY VISITOR: Prophesies never come true, but it's the intention that counts.

MISTRESS: To your health.

MASTER: [*after drinking*] Yes, to our health ... Even though at this point that word has about as much real meaning for me as El Dorado or Atlantis.

LADY VISITOR: Or Antonio.

MISTRESS: What are you talking about?

MASTER: I've wanted to tell you for some time now, but I haven't had the courage. You'll have to excuse me, because I'm going to ruin your evening, but I think the presence of these two new ... friends will help my wife and daughter to bear up. [*Overplaying the lines like a bad actor, he gets*

up and starts walking with a limp in the left leg.]
I have only a few months to live. I'm suffering
from a rare disease, and the doctor has told me
there's no hope.

MISTRESS: [*She does not know how to react. Inside, she is
pleased, because this way she can run off with the
love of her life.*] It's not ... possible. When did
you see the doctor? You've hardly been out of
the house ...

MASTER: You were sleeping. You didn't know a thing
about it. [*to the* DAUGHTER] And you had left for
those open spaces of yours.

DAUGHTER: But couldn't the doctor be wrong? Have you
consulted another one?

MASTER: I've seen several. They ran all the tests again,
and there's definitely no doubt about it. I am a
condemned man.

LADY VISITOR: [*with false piety*] But you won't be alone. Your
wife and your daughter will stay with you up
until the very end.

MISTRESS: Is that ... what you expect from us?

MASTER: Yes, and please [*He kneels before the* MISTRESS
and DAUGHTER, *who stand at his sides.*], on my
knees, I beg of you both, do not leave me alone
for a moment. Swear it to me, before these two
witnesses from God.

DAUGHTER: No! I can't swear it to you ... I'm sorry, but ...

MASTER: [*Unconvincingly, like a bad actor, he gets up and
starts limping heavily, this time on the right leg.*]
But why? ...

LADY VISITOR: [*in the* MASTER's *ear, whispering*] You're limping
on the wrong leg.

DAUGHTER: My dear foster father [*stroking his cheek with
great tenderness*], you're contradicting yourself.
Try to remember how one day you told me that
when you love someone, they cross over and

come to live inside you, because that's what love is, not being afraid of the other, feeling them as part of yourself, reconstructing them inside you. And that's why you will never die within me. You will go on living. I will remember you, and I will keep you healthy and vigorous inside me, so long as I live.

MASTER: [*half irritated, half disoriented*] I told you that?

DAUGHTER: Yes ... and I swear to you that I shall live. I'm brimming with life, intoxicated with it, and from this night on, I swear to burst each bubble of time in mad joy.

MISTRESS: *Mad* joy ...

DAUGHTER: Because ... why should I hide it from you any longer? He has come for me, and I'm not afraid of anyone anymore. [*points to the* LADY VISITOR] Not even of this woman who is trying to take him away from me ... because Antonio is here ... and he loves me ... [*She flings herself into the* VISITOR's *arms.*] as much as I love him! [*The* VISITOR *does not embrace her.*] Isn't it true? [*She sees that he does not react favorably, frightened as he is by the presence of the* LADY VISITOR.] Didn't you tell me that this very night we were going away together? The two of us, mounted on my horse, wrapped in each other's arms ...

MISTRESS: My child ... [*She takes her into her arms when the* DAUGHTER *lets go of the* VISITOR, *who has remained hieratically still.*] You are confused. And we are all to blame, we grown-ups. We thought it might be too strong an emotion for you, that it might produce too strong a jolt, to let you know ... that your real parents are alive ... They are, dear child, our visitors.

DAUGHTER: [*her mental balance greatly shaken*] What?

MISTRESS: He is your real father, and she your mother. But today you received the terrible news of your fiancé's breaking your engagement, so it's only natural that your mind is a little disturbed, and ... yes, you confused your father's effusiveness with something else ...

DAUGHTER: What do you know about what happened with my fiancé? What broken engagement? [*The* MASTERS *of the house exchange looks. The* DAUGHTER *points at the* VISITOR.] He is Antonio! And he has come back to take me away with him.

LADY VISITOR: My daughter ... we are your parents. Forgive us, but all these years, I promise you, it was we, your father and I, who suffered most from not being with you. But the fact is, we are ... two outlaws. Ours is a life of crime, and tonight we came here because the police are closing in on us. We are two burglars, and, if you don't believe us, the jewels from our last robbery are hidden in that sofa.

DAUGHTER: [*Feeling ill, nauseated, she leans on the* MISTRESS.] No. I don't know, madam, what you are talking about ...

LADY VISITOR: [*wickedly*] Don't call me that ... [*suddenly sincere, breaking up inside*] Call me ... by some other name ... [*The* VISITOR *has remained motionless, standing in the shadows.*]

MASTER: [*feeling emotion*] Call her ... by some other name.

DAUGHTER: [*very upset*] Some other name?

MASTER: Yes, let your own blood dictate the word to you.

DAUGHTER: Blood? ... Still more blood? ... I saw my own blood flow this afternoon ...

MASTER: That's all in your imagination.

107

LADY VISITOR: [to MASTER, MISTRESS, and VISITOR] Please, leave me alone for a few minutes ... with my daughter ...

DAUGHTER: No ... don't go away ...

MISTRESS: [giving her a kiss on the forehead and exiting stage left] Only for a moment ...

MASTER: We'll be right here, just a few feet away. [Also kisses her on the forehead and exits. The VISITOR looks at her, and the DAUGHTER looks back imploringly. He lowers his eyes and exits.]

LADY VISITOR: [very sincere, boldly] You had formed a very different picture ... of your mother? [takes her hand, kisses her, and leads her toward a chair] Please, sit down, completely calm, just for a moment, that's all ... [The DAUGHTER is so lost in the whirlpool of her thoughts that she lets herself be led to the chair and seats herself. The LADY VISITOR immediately kneels next to her, without letting go of her hand.] On the other hand, I had pictured you exactly like this—an angel. [She raises the DAUGHTER's hand to her cheek.] I know it's going to be very hard for you, in these circumstances, to grow fond of me. [The DAUGHTER continues not to respond, pausing.] In any situation, people have a hard time growing fond of me. [She is filled with emotion, her voice becomes veiled.] But in your case, perhaps, it would have been different ... Having you ever since you were little, day after day ... perhaps you really might have grown fond of me. I would have been your mama, the one who protected you from everything in the world ... [Her voice breaks with sobbing.] And that way, maybe, you wouldn't have been bothered by ... my power. How I envied that man, dying or not, when you told him you loved him, and that he'd live on forever within you! [*crying*] What a relief it would be to know that I am going to go on living, within another soul, fresh and pure as yours! Are you certain ... that it would be impossible for you to love me? [*Stepping silently, slowly, the* VISITOR *re-enters.*] The man [*The* LADY VISITOR *returns to being her brittle self.*] who came to be your father never loved me. [*becomes sincere again*] And I am weary of this—my destiny. I don't want to be me any longer ... Can't you understand that? You are so sensitive. Yes, you are beginning to understand me. And ... do you know? When you said that to love was to carry someone inside you, I thought that the day I die I might change myself into you ... you, whom everybody cares for, whom nobody fears ...

DAUGHTER: But you don't have to die. You're still young, and beautiful. My life with Antonio can't begin this way, with a death. My life with Antonio must be a model of perfection. We two will teach the world to be happy ...

LADY VISITOR: His name is not Antonio. He is your father.

DAUGHTER: You're trying to mix me up. [*She withdraws her hand from the* LADY VISITOR'*s.*] You are not my mother.

VISITOR: She is, and you must respect her, and obey her.

DAUGHTER: [*standing up and taking him by the arms*] Why do you say that? Why are you so afraid of her?

LADY VISITOR: There's no more time to lose. We have to get out of here. The police have lost our trail, and now we should get on with our plan.

VISITOR: We'll take her hostage.

DAUGHTER: No! You and I are the ones who have to run away together. Not her! [*The* VISITOR *covers her mouth with his hand.*]

LADY VISITOR: Yes. That way we'll be sure they won't call the police.

VISITOR: Give me that cloth so I can tie her hands. [*The* LADY VISITOR *hands him a long doily from one of the pieces of furniture.*] That goes here . . .

LADY VISITOR: Quick. [*They tie the* DAUGHTER'S *hands.*] And now her mouth . . . [*She finds another, similar furniture mat and hands it to the* VISITOR.] Here, take it. [*The* DAUGHTER *resists but they subdue her easily.*]

VISITOR: Where's the gun?

LADY VISITOR: In my purse, upstairs, with the rest of my clothes.

VISITOR: Go get it now . . . I'll take care of her . . . [*He throws her onto the sofa where they made love. The* DAUGHTER *cannot defend herself because her hands are tied behind her back. The* VISITOR *proceeds to search for another doily to bind her ankles.*] You never should have come down without the gun.

LADY VISITOR: It's well hidden. [*She looks upstairs, doesn't hear anything and begins to climb the stairs. When she is almost at the top, the* MISTRESS *appears at the head of the stairs, holding the gun, a pistol.*]

MISTRESS: Searching for this?

LADY VISITOR: [*to the* VISITOR] Look . . .

VISITOR: [*standing up, going toward the foot of the stairs*] Please, madam, be careful. The gun is loaded.

MISTRESS: [*looking at the* VISITOR] There's somebody one too many here.

LADY VISITOR: Put down that gun at once . . . lay it on the stairs . . .

MISTRESS [*to the* LADY VISITOR] Get down . . . out of my way . . .

LADY VISITOR: [*to the* VISITOR] Tell her to obey me.

MISTRESS: [*coming down the staircase, addressing the* VISITOR *with all the pent-up love of twenty years*] Please, I beg of you, don't make me wait any longer. Tell her you've come for me, and nothing else. She's going to understand. There's nothing else for her to do . . . Tell her—I am the strong one now, the gun's in my hand. We'll escape together. My car has a full tank of gas . . . but that must only have been an excuse for you to come after me . . . isn't that so? You couldn't bear another second without seeing me . . .

VISITOR: [*icily*] Madam, please. Just put down the gun, there, where she showed you.

MISTRESS: I'll kill her if it's necessary. You've no more reason to be afraid of her. Let's go now.

VISITOR: Put down the gun, there. It's loaded. [*firmly*] And I ask you, please, stop confusing me with someone I'm not. [*The* MISTRESS *fires a shot and the* VISITOR *falls dead.*]

LADY VISITOR: What have you done? [*She goes to the* VISITOR, *kneels, and takes him in her arms.*] It's not possible . . . he's dead . . .

MASTER: [*appears at the top of the stairs and addresses the* MISTRESS] Don't be afraid of anything. I'm right here beside you. [*to the* LADY VISITOR] And you, don't you be afraid either. I was your husband's best friend, and I'll go on protecting you every way I can.

LADY VISITOR: Protecting me? I despise you thoroughly. I've only known you for a few hours, and that's more than enough for me . . .

MISTRESS: You always were jealous of me, and with very good reason, as now you can see.

LADY VISITOR: You are a lunatic. Now, the only thing to do is load the corpse into the car. I'll take care of everything else. There's nothing left for you but to cooperate with me. Most of all, don't say a word to the police, because now you, madam, are just as much a criminal as I. We're on the same level. You'll have to cooperate whether you want to or not. The only important thing now is for neither of you to tell the police anything.

MISTRESS: His body belongs to me.

LADY VISITOR: [*to the* MASTER] There's no time to lose. That woman is insane. She's never seen this man before in her life. Take the gun away from her, now.

MISTRESS: Enough lies! [*fires at the* LADY VISITOR, *who falls dead*]

MASTER: [*walks slowly down to where the* LADY VISITOR *lies*] A body, right here, stretched out in the middle of the room, blocks the path.

DAUGHTER: [*making what sounds she can, bound and gagged as she is*] M-m-m-m-m.

MASTER: Child ... [*runs to her*] What you must have gone through! You, fragile as a flower, and in the middle of this witches' Sabbath.

MISTRESS: [*She has remained motionless, on the same step, midway down the flight of stairs.*] I have killed him.

MASTER: Correction. You have killed *them.*

DAUGHTER: [*freed from the gag while the* MASTER *goes about untying her hands and feet*] What madness ... [*deeply crushed*] Antonio hadn't done anything to you. Now life has no meaning for me.

MISTRESS: [*comes down the stairs slowly; places the pistol next to the* MASTER *and addresses him*] You were right ... this girl is deeply disturbed.

MASTER: Now's not the time for splitting hairs. [*to the* DAUGHTER] Help me get these two stumbling-blocks out of here. [*grabs the* LADY VISITOR *by the ankles*] Take hold of her hands.

DAUGHTER: My life has no meaning anymore.

MASTER: Help me, will you! [*The* DAUGHTER *obeys him.*]

MISTRESS: Don't let my robe drag. It's a souvenir from a trip. [MASTER *and* DAUGHTER *remove the* LADY VISITOR's *body, carrying her so as not to drag the robe. They exit stage left. The* MISTRESS *approaches the* VISITOR's *corpse, kneels beside him, raises his head, and kisses his lips.*] But to my life ... you did give meaning ... [*annihilated within*] and this is how I repay you ...

MASTER: [*reenters with the* DAUGHTER] For the time being they can stay in the pantry. Later they'll go to feed the furnace.

DAUGHTER: [*pouncing on the gun*] And me with them ...

MISTRESS: [*shouts*] No!

MASTER: [*quickly prevents the* DAUGHTER *from raising the gun to her breast*] Your life has hardly begun. [*takes the bullets out of the gun and puts them in his pocket*] What do you know about meaning? [*to the* MISTRESS] Let's see, help me get him out of here. I don't like having my best friend sprawled out on the floor this way. [*The* MISTRESS *grasps the* VISITOR's *hands and the* MASTER *his feet. They can't lift him.*]

DAUGHTER: It's useless. He was a giant.

MISTRESS: With muscles like granite.

MASTER: Nonsense. It's his conscience that weighs so heavily. [*The* MASTER *pulls the rug on which the corpse is lying and succeeds in taking it out stage left, just like the* LADY VISITOR's.]

DAUGHTER: [*begins to smooth her clothes, to fix her hair, still in a trance of deep confusion*] But now ... we're three killers ... [*The* MASTER *and* MISTRESS *reenter.*] We're accomplices to a crime.

MASTER: No, my pet. The two of us are innocent. [*points*

113

to the MISTRESS] She's the only guilty party: first an adulterous wife and now a murderess ...

MISTRESS: No. The three of us, we did it together, by mutual consent, and in self-defense ...

MASTER: Let's hear none of that. You pulled the trigger all by yourself. I only loaded the revolver and left it within your reach ...

MISTRESS: It's a plot ...

MASTER: Hadn't you caught on yet? Ah, but how well everything has turned out. The unfaithful wife who eliminates her lover, and, with a single bullet—or, should I say two?—steps out of the way, leaving her husband to start his life all over ... [*addresses the* DAUGHTER] Because life has more than one meaning ... and I take it upon myself to teach you that. [*takes hold of her by the arms*] I'm not your father, and I won't be master of this house either. I'll simply be a man you love ...

DAUGHTER: Yes, I already love you, with all my heart and soul, but in another way ...

MASTER: I'll teach you to love me in a thousand ways.

DAUGHTER: She killed Antonio.

MASTER: She killed your parents.

DAUGHTER: Please, I can't stand it anymore. Take me away from here.

MASTER: [*embraces her and quickly kisses her on the lips*] I knew you'd understand. Let's get going. [*to the* MISTRESS] And you, get busy so nobody discovers what happened this afternoon. You know, everything into the furnace :.. And afterwards, silence. I'll move the convertible away from the house.

DAUGHTER: Let's leave in it ... but, please, as fast as possible. I'm afraid that something even worse is going to happen tonight.

MASTER: All right ... my dear. And once in the city, we'll get rid of the car ... Let's go now.

MISTRESS: No. Please. Don't leave me here alone ... [*The doorbell rings.*]

MASTER: That must be the maid.

DAUGHTER: Don't open the door.

MASTER: No, that way she might suspect something.

MISTRESS: [*to the* MASTER] You open it, please. [*The* MASTER *opens the front door and the* DOCTOR *and* NURSE, *in their appropriate professional outfits, appear. They are played by the same actors who played the* VISITORS, *but he no longer wears a beard or mustache.*]

DOCTOR: Good evening.

MASTER: What can I do for you?

DOCTOR: Are you the man of the house?

MASTER: [*After a moment's hesitation, he answers with difficulty.*] Yes ...

MISTRESS: [*from where she stands, without moving*] And I am his wife. Won't you please come in?

DOCTOR: [*enters with the nurse*] Thank you.

MASTER: [*Gaining more confidence, he takes a step toward the* DOCTOR *and* NURSE.] And this is our adopted daughter.

DOCTOR: Very well, then. This morning the Municipal Psychiatric Hospital received a typical call from a family in an emergency situation. The call for help was cut off, but in such cases we systematically trace the call through the operator.

MASTER: It was a foolish thing, actually ... We were worried about ... the disappearance [*points to the* DAUGHTER] of our daughter.

NURSE: [*hastily approaches the* DAUGHTER] The young lady needs help?

DAUGHTER: No ... actually, I was leaving the house, with him. In order to begin a new life, as he put it. 115

No. He said, "Free to start our lives all over again." [*taking the* MASTER's *arm*] Please, tell them, so they stop looking at me that way.

MISTRESS: But, silly, what's this about wanting to go away from here? And your father, why do you want to take him away from his home, where he has all his papers? Remember: he's writing his memoirs . . .

NURSE: [*Seeing that the* DAUGHTER *drops the* MASTER's *arm, she approaches the* DAUGHTER *and takes her by the arm.*] You really do need help, don't you?

MASTER: If you want their help, just ask. Would you rather we left you alone with these people?

DAUGHTER: [*looks at the* MASTER] That depends on you. Tell me now: what do I have to do?

MASTER: Talk with them, if that seems right to you. We grown-ups might be in your way. [*to the* MISTRESS] Better to leave them alone, don't you think?

DAUGHTER: [*leaves no time for the* MISTRESS *to respond*] But only with the doctor . . . no one else.

NURSE: [*barely masks her annoyance*] I can leave, of course.

MASTER: [*points to the exit, stage left*] Let's go this way, then.

MISTRESS: [*remembering that they will find the two bodies that way*] No, dear. Not that way. Everything's a mess out there. [*points upstairs*] Let's go up to your study.

MASTER: You're right. [*to the* NURSE] This way . . .

NURSE: Thank you. [*Halfway up the stairs with the* MASTER *and the* MISTRESS, *she speaks to the* DOCTOR.] But don't forget, Doctor, we still have other calls to make, before midnight.

DOCTOR: OK. I'll keep it in mind. [*The* NURSE, MASTER,

of ... that one day they'd take her away like
this.

MISTRESS: [*very sad*] Poor thing.

MASTER: [*collapsing within*] What a day!

MISTRESS: The joy she brought us was too great. We
couldn't bear it, and on our own we began
imagining difficulties. From that point to their
coming about was a short step.

MASTER: [*drops into one of the chairs, leaning his head onto
the arm*] Tonight our old age begins. Can't you
feel it?

MISTRESS: Yes, but I couldn't have put it in such precise
terms.

MASTER: Our two best friends are shot, dead. We didn't
know how to understand them. And our
daughter is on her way to a ward for the dis-
traught.

MISTRESS: At least our old age may be ... short.

MASTER: Every minute will be a torment.

MISTRESS: May heaven take pity on us ... and finish this
quickly.

MASTER: Our old age *could* be ... short.

MISTRESS: You'd take care of it yourself?

MASTER: Yes. You only have to ask me ...

MISTRESS: I don't have the courage ... but you have
enough for both of us, don't you?

MASTER: I will be the executor, but you tell me how,
when ...

MISTRESS: [*interrupting*] Now ...

MASTER: But tell me how ... [*He puts the gun to her tem-
ple, and the doorbell rings.*]

MISTRESS: Who could that be? Don't open the door!

MASTER: Maybe it's that ... clown, that quack again.
Better open the door and get rid of him fast.

MISTRESS: [*goes to the door, coquettish again, fixing her hair*]
In that case, I'll go ... [*She opens the door, and*

in the shadow there stands a girl, modestly dressed in gray clothes that might be confused with a maid's uniform. The character is played by the same actress who played the DAUGHTER.] What can I do for you?

MAID: [*very animated but extremely humble, almost servile*] I'm the person who's going to do things for you, madam.

MASTER: The maid!

MAID: [*enters and curtsies*] The one and only!

MISTRESS: [*half satisfied, half disoriented*] But at this hour . . .

MAID: I beg your pardon, a thousand times, but I got lost . . . For hours and hours, I've been circling around in these fields. [*looks around the room, ecstatic*] What an inviting place!

MISTRESS: It's a little messy.

MASTER: Yes. There are some rooms you can't even go into, until morning.

MISTRESS: Yes, and the truth is . . . maybe we don't need your services anymore.

MAID: Oh! . . . What a pity that would be . . . because I was hardly in the door before I felt something special about this house.

MASTER: [*ill at ease*] For example . . . ?

MAID: I felt that this was . . . a real home.

MISTRESS: Why?

MAID: Well . . . I'm not the best person to explain that. I never had a home. I'm an orphan. But I'd always pictured a home exactly this way.

MASTER: What way?

MAID: This way, with the gentleman of the house very intelligent, a writer maybe . . . and the lady very elegant, who leaves her mark on everything she touches. This flower arrangement, for instance.

MISTRESS: [*flattered*] But this is an out-of-the-way place, not for young people.

MAID: That's what I like about it—it's so peaceful. And when I want to hear other voices, I can always turn on the radio.

MASTER: You like music?

MAID: Crazy about it. Not so much the serials though, except for one, at ten o'clock. I never miss that.

MISTRESS: Well, we missed it last night.

MAID: I heard it!

MISTRESS: I can't believe it!

MAID: Yes, and I can tell you the story, if you want me to . . .

MASTER: It's 9:30. We could have a bite to eat while you tell us.

MISTRESS: And at 10, we can hear today's episode.

MAID: I can stay then?

MISTRESS: [*to the* MASTER] What do you think?

MASTER: She could . . . stay, don't you think so?

MISTRESS: I think so too . . . [*to the* MAID] Stay!

MAID: [*deeply moved*] Madam [*sighs in relief*], what a relief! I thought all this [*indicating the house*] was only a dream, and that all of a sudden I'd wake up, all alone again, in the darkness of the countryside.

MISTRESS: Well, if it makes you happy . . . stay . . .

MAID: [*kisses the* MISTRESS' *hand, then the* MASTER'S] Thank you . . . thank you! And now I'm going to straighten up all this.

MISTRESS: All right. [*The* MAID *sets about putting things in order. First she puts the doilies in their proper places, as if well acquainted with them, and then brings to fluff the cushions.*] In the meantime, I'll fix a little refreshment.

MASTER: [*moves to extreme stage left, down to the footlights*]   **121**

Listen [*starts to smile*], you've caught on, haven't you?

MISTRESS: [*feigning, watching over her shoulder, to make sure that the* MAID *can not hear them as she arranges the room*] No. Caught on to what?

MASTER: It's her ... It's another one of her pranks ...

MAID: Whose?

MASTER: Our child. She's come back. We haven't lost her.

MISTRESS: [*remote*] Do you think so?

MASTER: Yes, I'm sure.

MISTRESS: What makes you say so?

MASTER: Simply ... because our luck couldn't have been that bad. She didn't lose her mind, they didn't take her away to the psychiatric pavilion. She's here, playing with us, just the way she did when she was a little girl.

MISTRESS: It's true. We never deserved such bad luck.

MASTER: And everything else was pure fear, pure imagination. There, in that room, there are no two corpses, shot to death, on the floor. You didn't kill anyone.

MISTRESS: Of course I didn't kill anyone ... Me? A murderess? Me? Who all my life have been a peaceful housewife and music lover?

MASTER: A housewife, with a deep secret, always waiting for the miracle to repeat itself.

MISTRESS: [*half surprised, half pleased*] You knew all along ... [*snuggles in his arms, looking up*]

MASTER: Yes ...

MISTRESS: I never stopped waiting for him. I never believed he could have died that way, so stupidly, in an automobile accident back in 1929.

MASTER: And now ... you're still waiting for him?

MISTRESS: Yes ...

MASTER: And I'm not going to leave you alone for a second. The minute I see him arrive, I'll fight, right up to the end, for what I love most. I'll defend myself somehow ... I'll kill him if necessary. [*At this point, the* MAID *discovers the bag of jewels under the cushion. She opens it and begins to examine the contents, dazzled. The* MASTER *and* MISTRESS, *lost in their joy, are not aware of her.*]

MISTRESS: None of that, now. Everything will be arranged in a quite gentlemanly manner.

MASTER: You think so?

MISTRESS: Yes ... you let yourself get carried away by your imagination. Today we've already killed two people in our delirium.

MAID: There's something hidden here, a bag of jewels.

MASTER: [*amused at the prospect of the game, but not looking at the* MAID] Aha! ... You don't say so? Isn't that fun?

MAID: But, sir ... they look real.

MISTRESS: In this house everything is legitimate, starting with our desires.

MAID: But, madam ...

MASTER: Just like before ... [*The* MAID, *frightened by the eccentricities of her employers, tiptoes to the door. Then she looks back and sees the bag of jewels again. Suddenly she feels tempted to go back and get it. She does so, hiding it among the pleats of her uniform. She approaches the door stealthily and finally escapes.*]

MASTER: [*to the* MISTRESS *with his back turned to the* MAID] As you can see ... there are no dead bodies in the pantry, and our girl has come back. At this very moment, she is not terrified in her dungeon. She's with her parents, who adore her.

MISTRESS: But such waiting, so many anxieties.

MASTER: And if you had to do it all over again, just in

order to achieve this moment of peace? If that were the price of this peace?

MISTRESS: This isn't a moment of peace. It's a moment of renewed hope, for his return.

MASTER: I'll fight for what's mine.

MISTRESS: [*flirtatious*] I thought I didn't interest you any longer . . .

MASTER: If he comes back for you, that means you're valuable, that you're worth a lot.

MISTRESS: A moment ago, I thought I wanted to die, but it wasn't true. Only weariness, and now that's passed. And, yes, I'd do it all over again. Everything—endless waiting, horrible anxieties—everything, just so I feel that joy again, one more time.

MASTER: Don't talk so loud, the child might hear you.

MISTRESS: [*in hushed tones*] That joy. That joy he brought me, those afternoons.

MASTER: [*also in hushed tones*] But afterwards? Afternoons are short, they end quickly.

MISTRESS: Afterwards comes the night, and I shut my eyes in peace, under a mantle of stars. [*A police siren is heard.*]

MASTER: A police siren! And it's heading this way . . .

MISTRESS: No! It's going farther out. Don't panic. God only knows where it's headed . . . [*They both listen.*]

MASTER: No, they're coming here. [*The siren sounds nearer.*] And they're looking for us.

MISTRESS: Nonsense. It couldn't be. Not now, when you desire me the way you once did.

MASTER: You're right. [*Car doors are heard slamming.*]

MISTRESS: No. It couldn't possibly be. Don't open the door!

MASTER: No! [*embraces her tightly*] I promise you. This time I won't. [*The doorbell rings loudly.*]

MASTER: It's the door.

VOICE OF
POLICEMAN: Surround the place, nobody gets out alive.

MISTRESS: [*seeing the* MASTER *about to open the door*] Don't! [*He opens it.*]

POLICEMAN: [*the same actor who played the* VISITOR, *now wearing a police uniform*] Sir, madam ... good evening.

MASTER: [*pretending to be calm*] Good evening.

MISTRESS: [*terrified*] Good evening.

POLICEMAN: My pals and I were worried about you. Everything pointed to this house being invaded by two dangerous criminals.

MISTRESS: [*admiring the* POLICEMAN'S *manner*] That's so, but I eliminated them.

MASTER: They're in the pantry, dead.

POLICEMAN: What an extraordinary feat!

MASTER: Executed by my wife. She is a very brave woman.

POLICEMAN: As nimble-fingered as she's elegant, if I may say so.

MASTER: As nimble-fingered as she is elegant ... and watched over by her husband, who happens to be me.

MISTRESS: What a good feeling, knowing you're protected by law and order, symbolized by you.

POLICEMAN: [*flattered*] Me? A symbol of order?

MISTRESS: Of order, and of something more. If it weren't for that uniform, I could easily take you for someone else ... someone I loved a lot.

MASTER: But dear ... this man is an agent of the police ...

MISTRESS: It doesn't matter who he is, it matters how he is.

POLICEMAN: [*fascinated*] And just how am I? I always wanted to know.

MISTRESS: [*romantically*] You are ... exactly the way I imagined you.

CURTAIN

MYSTERY
OF THE
ROSE
BOUQUET

TRANSLATED BY
ALLAN BAKER

Mystery of the Rose Bouquet was first performed at the Donmar Warehouse on 24 July 1987. The cast was as follows:

PATIENT: Brenda Bruce
NURSE: Gemma Jones

Act One

A private room in an exclusive clinic. The PATIENT *is lying in bed. It is a bright sunny day. The curtains are drawn. Very little light spills into the room.*

The PATIENT, *white-haired, wears a glazed, distant expression; her eyes are red from weeping.*

A NURSE *stands watching the* PATIENT. *The* PATIENT *is totally still. The* NURSE *approaches her and smoothes the bedspread; waits for a reaction. There is none. Suddenly, she gathers her courage and goes to the* PATIENT'*s night table. With extreme care she opens the drawer and takes out two pill bottles.*

> PATIENT: [*a bundle of nerves, explodes*] Put those back!
> [*She grabs them from the* NURSE'*s hand.*]

NURSE: [*frightened by the sudden reaction of the* PATIENT] *I'm sorry.*

PATIENT: Those are my barbiturates.

NURSE: I'll take your tray now, shall I?

[*The* PATIENT *doesn't answer. The* NURSE *leans across and sees the food hasn't been touched.*]

Aren't you going to eat any more?

[*The* PATIENT *looks at her, saying nothing.*]

So I can take it away then?

PATIENT: The doctor didn't explain my case?

NURSE: [*compliant yet maintaining her dignity*] I'm sorry, señora.

PATIENT: So you're not a qualified nurse?

NURSE: Now I come to think of it, the doctor did mention that you only picked at your food, yes.

PATIENT: I don't touch it. I can't stand the sight of it.

NURSE: Then I'll take it away. Perhaps you'd prefer something to drink instead?

PATIENT: I shall have some tea at five. Didn't the doctor explain that either?

NURSE: Yes. Now I remember.

PATIENT: You're forgetful.

NURSE: No, it's not that exactly.

PATIENT: [*sarcastic*] Then what is it—*exactly?*

NURSE: I don't know. Maybe it's just first-day nerves.

PATIENT: I'm the one in here for nerves. One is quite enough.

NURSE: You're right, of course.

PATIENT: [*curt*] Sit down. Just what did the doctor tell you, about me?

NURSE: [*shifting on her feet; she doesn't sit*] This and that.

PATIENT: [*Irritated, she shouts gruffly.*] Sit down. [*Sees that she has now scared the* NURSE, *who has now sat down.*] Sorry, I didn't mean to make you nervous.

NURSE: The doctor said that you had suffered a misfortune. This had left you in a depression. You've grown quite weak, and they had to put you in the clinic.

PATIENT: They had to put me in the clinic!! I did it!! I came of my own free will.

NURSE: Oh, yes, I knew that. Your daughter wanted you to stay with her.

PATIENT: And did he get round to telling you why I refuse to be attended by the clinic's own staff?

NURSE: Not really . . .

PATIENT: The nurses here are badly paid, and I wish to be well cared for. That's why you're paid what you are.

NURSE: I'm most grateful.

PATIENT: And I should be grateful to you if you didn't mix with the other employees here. Just behave as if we were in my home.

NURSE: Excuse me, señora, but there were other things the doctor didn't explain . . . and . . . I suppose it's my fault for not asking, but . . . well, why aren't we in your home anyway?

PATIENT: The man is an idiot. I made the decision to come here because I have no desire to depart this life from lack of medical attention. It's not that living is anything special. But I certainly shan't die from neglect. I'll die soon enough but not from neglect.

[*Silence. The* NURSE *doesn't know how to respond. The* PATIENT *continues, increasingly irritated.*]

How are your nerves now?

NURSE: [*after a delay*] Still on edge . . . but less than before.

PATIENT: Well, this might just push them over the brink. [*Pause.*] You are the fourth nurse I've engaged

131

this week alone, and I'll let you in on a secret. Nothing makes me more nervous than people with short memories!

NURSE: But I don't have a short memory. On the contrary, I never forget anything. It's a real affliction at times.

PATIENT: Afflictions are my prerogative. You're not being paid to burden me with your own. [*Pause.*] Besides, you really can't expect me to have sympathy given how I'm being sucked dry by that union of yours. Every time I fire one of you, I have to pay a week's notice, pension fund and a Christmas bonus too, I shouldn't be surprised.

NURSE: [*hesitates*] The doctor did say something . . . but he told me not to mention it to you . . .

PATIENT: Not mention it to me! What was it?

NURSE: It seemed rather complicated.

PATIENT: [*curious*] Well, you have to tell me now. I insist.

NURSE: The doctor didn't want to take me on at first. Because of my nursing diploma . . . in fact, I don't actually have one, but as I've already got so many years of service, the union have given me a card. But I never properly studied.

PATIENT: [*ironic*] This sounds promising. Go on.

NURSE: The doctor said I'd be on probation. You see, I begged him to take me on because I need the money.

PATIENT: Someone who needs the money! How original!

NURSE: It's true—I'm on probation. If you don't eat anything within two days, I'm out on the street again.

PATIENT: [*sarcastic*] You've still got a day left.

NURSE: He said if I could manage to distract you, you might start eating without noticing it.

PATIENT: I've got bad news for you. Every day food revolts me more.

NURSE: [*after a pause*] Yes, well, don't worry about it, señora. The truth is . . . I never expected to last long anyhow.

PATIENT: What else did that fool of a doctor tell you?

NURSE: Not much. I suppose he thought I wouldn't be here long enough for it to matter. Of course, he did say yours was an acute depression, although you weren't prone to such things.

PATIENT: Not prone to such things! What utter rubbish! You might as well hear it from me. It's been almost fourteen months now since my grandson died in a car accident. He was only twenty-two. It'll be fourteen months exactly on the ninth. My only daughter, she had an only child who was . . . he was everything one could ask for. My daughter felt awful at first, but she's never been capable of deep feelings. As soon as she grew bored with her first husband, she went off with someone else. So the boy came and lived with me. I was more of a mother to him than she was. Now she's found herself another candidate. She hasn't even bothered going to the altar with this one.

NURSE: What was he called, your grandson?

PATIENT: [*trying to restrain her emotions*] He *is* called Victor. One shouldn't ever say "was" called. He hasn't lost his name. On the contrary, his name is all that's left, as wrapping for all the memories. His name is Victor.

NURSE: Did he have a girlfriend?
[*Pause.*]

PATIENT: Yes . . . and in this instance it's quite correct to say "had." Because he doesn't have her any-

more. She got married only last month. And
we thought she'd never get over Victor's death.
We were all scared at first because she wouldn't
get out of bed after Victor died. I even went to
their apartment on my own to see her—at my
age. It cut me to the quick to come face to face
with Victor's personal things. But I did it. You
see, I was afraid the girl might do something
foolish to herself ... and the child, if she was
carrying one. I was frightened she'd do it. I
begged her to have the baby. I gave her my
solemn word I would provide for both of them,
that she would never have to worry about anything, but ... she wasn't pregnant. [*Pause.*]
When she went back to her parents, she cleared
all her things out of the apartment. No one had
it in them to see to Victor's things. I went and
dealt with it all myself. I still had my strength
at that time. But soon afterwards I began to feel
unwell ... I've never gotten over it.

NURSE: I have an idea, señora, although I don't know
whether you'll approve of it or not.

PATIENT: What is it?

NURSE: I hope you won't think I'm being forward. But
if you let me eat your food, the doctor would
think *you* had eaten it and then I could stay one
more day.

PATIENT: [*cross*] You're going to stuff yourself? On top of
your lunch?

NURSE: I've hardly had a bite to eat all day. I have to
eat in the visitors' canteen, and there was a
queue. And besides, it's very expensive there.

PATIENT: You can't eat stone-cold food, it'll make you ill.
Don't touch it.

NURSE: I could just try a forkful ... won't you let
me?

PATIENT: No. It would be deceiving the doctor. I can't condone that.

NURSE: You're quite right. I shouldn't have mentioned it.

PATIENT: [*after a pause*] If you're hungry, I can order something for you.

NURSE: No. Thank you. Ordering extra food is an extravagance. I know. I've seen the price list.

PATIENT: [*drily*] I can afford it. Money's no problem.

NURSE: I'm very grateful . . . but I'll only accept what's here on the tray. Nothing else.

PATIENT: Be my guest. Poison yourself. [*She gestures to the tray.*]

NURSE: Thank you. [*She begins eating.*]

PATIENT: If you clean the plate, the doctor will become suspicious, won't he?

NURSE: The bread roll is delicious. Crusty.

PATIENT: I didn't even bother to see what it was. What is it?

NURSE: A nice chicken breast with mashed potatoes and salad. And stewed apples.

PATIENT: There can be no doubt. We really are in a hospital.

NURSE: It's not bad at all.

PATIENT: I don't wish to hear about it. The mere mention of food disgusts me.

[*Black-out.*]

L ight change. The following night. A standard lamp illuminates the room.

PATIENT: [*almost sitting up in bed: she has raised herself a little higher since the last scene*] The lawyer's telephone number is in my little address book. You'll find it in my handbag in the cupboard. Don't forget to make a note of it.

NURSE: [*sitting on a regular hospital chair; she makes herself comfortable, a notepad in one hand and a pencil in the other*] What shall I say?

PATIENT: [*dictating, her eyes looking at the ceiling*] Indefinitely postpone sale of the Arribenos Street apartment dash dash until my health comma God willing comma will permit me to oversee negotiations myself full stop. [*She looks at the* NURSE.] You can telephone him in the morning from the kiosk in the hallway so you won't disturb me. Make sure you speak to him in person, don't let them fob you off with any of that "I'll see he gets the message" nonsense.

NURSE: You're very experienced at running things. I can tell.

PATIENT: I don't relish giving orders.
[*Pause.*]

NURSE: But you know how to give them. And make them clear.

PATIENT: [*less sharply*] I'm not one of those women who like behaving like a man. I've been quite content just being a housewife. I loved cooking. I've always considered it the most creative part of managing a home, don't you agree?

NURSE: Without a doubt...

PATIENT: I was never keen on housework. But I was always fortunate enough to afford a maid. And you? Do you enjoy looking after your home?

NURSE: I don't know. I've always had to go out to work. I've not had the time to find much satisfaction in it.

PATIENT: Who looks after your home, then?

NURSE: My mother used to do it all. But she passed away last year.

PATIENT: In which month?

NURSE: In August. The same month as your grandson. Your doctor told me.

PATIENT: *When* did he tell you this?

NURSE: When he interviewed me. I think that's why he gave me the job, because both of us suffered our bereavements at the same time.

PATIENT: The man is a fool. What has one got to do with the other? One of them was on the threshold of his life. How old was your mother?

NURSE: Seventy-one. And I'm nearly forty-eight.

PATIENT: But you're not alone.

NURSE: You have your daughter.

PATIENT: That's the same as being alone. Whom do you have?

NURSE: Nobody.

PATIENT: [*almost mocking*] A spinster. Nevertheless, you could still marry ... [*more mocking*] ... You're not *too* old.

NURSE: I'm separated. It's been a couple of years now. I don't think I'll ever marry anyone else, or find the right man to suit me.

PATIENT: The first one suited you fine and turned out no good. Why be fussy? Marry anyone.

NURSE: I'd like a different sort of life. Not a house-wife's life.

PATIENT: [*annoyed and annoying*] So you prefer to be a nurse and look after unbearable people such as me. There's no accounting for tastes.

NURSE: I like medicine. I always liked it but I never had the opportunity to study properly. I barely finished primary school.

PATIENT: [*with growing anger which she cannot contain*] If you never studied, it's clearly because you didn't want to. You could have gone to night school.

137

NURSE: It's true. I didn't think I had it up here.

PATIENT: And now you regret it.

NURSE: I'll go to my grave regretting it.

PATIENT: [*gruffly, annoyed with this topic*] Blaming yourself for it all.

NURSE: How did you guess that?

PATIENT: [*Impatient, she looks at her watch.*] It's coming up to six thirty. Have your dinner now and come back later.

NURSE: I'll wait until you've had yours first.

PATIENT: No. I know you'll be making eyes at my tray. You go now.

NURSE: As you wish—I'll come back later, señora. [*She waits to see if the* PATIENT *will acknowledge her departure—she won't.*]

PATIENT: Before you go. I do not want you removing my barbiturates from this table again. Put them back immediately.

NURSE: Of course. [*She crosses to the wardrobe.*]

PATIENT: And I'm not suicidal. I'm not like that. If I ever did want to do something like that, then it's my business entirely. But I shan't be treated like a child.

NURSE: Here you are. [*Apprehensive, she hands her the pill bottles.*]

PATIENT: Why such a fuss? They won't burn you.

NURSE: I don't approve of barbiturates, they're so powerful . . . All it needs is a little carelessness . . .

PATIENT: Carelessness doesn't enter into it. If you want to kill yourself, you turn on the tap, fill a glass with water, turn off the tap, swallow a handful of tablets. What do you mean, careless?

NURSE: They are dangerous. Some people don't have your self-control.

PATIENT: [*interrupting*] You don't know what you're talking about. Now leave me. Go.

NURSE: Very well. I won't be long. [*She leaves.*]

[*The* PATIENT *tries to settle down in bed, but she is overcome with a sudden anxiety. She lets out a scream and curls up in bed. The lights dim, the* PATIENT *slips her feet from under the covers and places them on the floor. The wardrobe lights up and the door opens slowly.*]

PATIENT: [*She looks down at her feet and ignores the wardrobe.*] So many things swimming around in one's head ... What use is it being able to remember so much?

[*The* NURSE *steps out of the wardrobe. A ghostly light circles her. One at a time she removes grips holding her cap in place. She speaks in her usual manner.*]

NURSE: Maybe the forgotten things would be the really useful ones.

PATIENT: [*Without looking up, she talks ironically, almost parodying her own nostalgia.*] Each time I think of you you're in your fox stole and that hat with a cluster of cherries ... How we used to enjoy making our own hats!

NURSE: [*neither nostalgic nor sentimental*] It's true, it was fun, both sisters concocting those fake cherries.

PATIENT: [*still ironic*] Dark red cellophane paper, blood-red, and cotton-wool stuffing. [*She takes a clothes stand from inside the wardrobe—the old-fashioned type with flutes and curlicues on which hang a hat with cherries and a silver fox fur stole.*] I'm going to put the hat on your head. I remember just the way you used to pull it right down over your forehead. What fun!

NURSE: You can remember it now because you're asleep, but when you wake up you won't remember anything. Pity.

[*The* PATIENT, *nimble as a thirty-year-old, stands* 139

up. For the first time she looks at the NURSE. *She picks up the hat and puts it on the* NURSE'*s head.*]

PATIENT: There ... that's the way ... perfect.

NURSE: [*Her tone changes totally, it becomes familiar, natural and warm.*] That's it, exactly ... [*She puts on the fur stole.*] Is this how I used to wear it?

PATIENT: Just so. [*adjusting the hat*] And with the brim just off the forehead with your hair swept back to show off your profile and that pert little nose of yours.

NURSE: I was always the more attractive. But you never minded. Well, how could you have?

PATIENT: You won't believe this, but I've forgotten why not.

NURSE: Because you went to college and I didn't!

PATIENT: Listen, Dora. I can remember so many wonderful things when I'm asleep like now, after taking a couple of my pills and dozing on my pillow. But as soon as I open my eyes—it's all gone. Nothing. It makes me so cross.

NURSE: That's just what I've been saying. Well, here I am paying you a visit and parched as well. Where's the tea trolley? Get on with it!
[*The* PATIENT *takes a little tea trolley on castors from the wardrobe with everything all laid out.*]

PATIENT: It's all ready! You're always in such a hurry. [*She wheels the trolley between the two chairs. Speaks affectionately.*] And now you tell me something. Why didn't you continue with your studies?

NURSE: Good heavens! There's no mystery. There just wasn't enough money at home to pay for both of us. And you were the bright one. [*rebuking with her little finger*] And, by the way, there was no such thing as night school in those days.

PATIENT: [*innocently*] And why did I bother with all that

studying only to end up getting married? It was all pointless.

NURSE: Well, you weren't as pretty as I was, of course. But for some reason the boys still wouldn't leave you alone. [*She stands up and takes a picture hat from the clothes stand.*] You used to wear a hat even to college. [*She studies the picture hat, figuring how to put it on her sister's head.*]

PATIENT: Put it on properly, be careful.

NURSE: The thing is that the one who studied didn't need a career after all, while I did. [*She places the picture hat on the* PATIENT's *head.*] I had to put up with working in an office for four years, typing away with my two fingers. I never stopped blaming you for my back pains.

PATIENT: But later on you got married too.

NURSE: But I should have so much liked the chance to have an education. It made me so angry when my children went to your house with their homework. They never thought I might know the answers. *Just* you. [*serious*] It isn't fair! I should have gone to university too!

PATIENT: Don't be cross with me, Dora. We'll have a good long chat about it all one of these days when I'm awake. With mother too.

NURSE: It'd be for the best to speak with each other quite candidly, not hold things in because that's bad for you.

PATIENT: [*with deep sadness and candor*] But ... Dora, mother is dead. We can't sort things out with her now.

NURSE: And I'm dead too, or have you forgotten that?

PATIENT: [*straightforwardly*] Well, yes, but I so wanted us to have a leisurely chat that it quite slipped my mind.

NURSE: Very well, I'll pour while you get on with tell-

ing me those pressing matters that I had to
drop everything to come and listen to. It had
better be good.

PATIENT: Oh, Dora. It's so hard to know where to begin.
And today my little daughter has her French
class, otherwise she'd be home by now, and
then we wouldn't be able to talk.

NURSE: Stop beating around the bush. I'm listening.

PATIENT: [*with a huge effort*] The world has collapsed
around my ears, Dora . . . Louis doesn't care for
me anymore.

NURSE: What makes you say that?

PATIENT: Well, it's been a while since he . . . you know,
even though he wants to, he can't always manage to . . . I mean, to be a husband to me. And
then he told me he's been seeing another
woman. He told me everything.

NURSE: And have you said anything about this to
mamma?

PATIENT: Yes—so you needn't play-act with me . . . she
said that the two of you suspected as much
already, but you didn't want to break the bad
news to me . . . And now I want to get a separa-
tion but mamma says I should wait, Louis will
get over this in time. But I want to go my own
way. I'll find a job. I have my law qualifications. [*She tries to soften her tone.*] Why should I
stay cooped up in here all day if things don't
work anymore?

NURSE: Louis is a good man. You won't find another
like him easily.

PATIENT: All I want is a good job and my little girl.

NURSE: If you want my advice—just grin and bear it.
Be patient. It'd be a terrible blow to mamma.
And as for your daughter—they'll never let you

keep her ... [*persuasive*] In your position, I'd sit tight and wait.

PATIENT: The thing is I've always loved Louis ... [*finally opening up without reticence*] But now I don't know if I do anymore. He's always so tense. God forbid things aren't done the way he wants. I don't count for anything in this house.

NURSE: Don't talk nonsense. Tell me just one thing he's ever denied you? He's on edge like any businessman these days. Believe me, dear, at the end of a hard day what a husband wants is to come home to peace and quiet. Now, you have to admit, you're not the most relaxing of people even at the best of times; you're always fussing about that little girl, either there's been ructions at school or she's running a temperature. Of course, that's you all over, bossy and a bag of nerves at the same time. But the man is the head of the family, and that's a big responsibility on Louis's shoulders and he needs some understanding.

[*She helps herself to another cup of tea.*]

PATIENT: But I want to try ... another kind of life, more independent. I'm sure I'd do well as a lawyer.

NURSE: Well, do whatever you want. [*She holds the* PATIENT*'s hand affectionately.*] But it's something different you must try to change: be easy on him, don't make demands. You can bet this other woman yesses him all the time and doesn't make any demands.

PATIENT: So you agree with mamma ...

NURSE: [*standing*] I *do* understand, there can be moments when a woman feels humiliated, when a man walks all over her. But a false sense of pride is not the answer. [*She goes to the door.*] A woman has a duty to be understand-ing, that's my opinion. [*She opens the door to leave the room.*]

PATIENT: [*stands up, seething with anger*] And I just kept my mouth shut and listened to your advice. You stupid old-fashioned idiot! Didn't it ever cross your mind that a woman could have dig-nity too? That man was betraying me with another woman, and on top of that he was a beast at home.

NURSE: [*affecting ignorance*] You'll make me late. I must be on my way now.

PATIENT: You're better off dead so you don't see the mess you've caused with your ignorant advice.

NURSE: I'm your sister. You have no right to speak to me like that!

PATIENT: [*mocking, wounding*] Oh, it's as plain as that nose of yours you never had an education.

NURSE: [*returning the insult*] And a lot of good yours did you!

PATIENT: [*pulling off the bonnet*] You won't be needing this back in the graveyard either! It's pointless my talking to you, there's no time left now to change anything. If you could only see what women these days are doing for themselves! [*She returns towards the center of the room as if talking to herself.*] False pride! Stupid bitch! But I'm not blaming you, I saw things weren't going well. Why didn't I ever bother opening my mouth to complain? . . . I lacked the guts to fight for my point of view, that's the sad truth. But how dear I paid! [*She turns again on her opponent with renewed anger.*] If you were alive, I'd wring your neck! [*She tries to take away the fox stole*] I'm going to strangle you with that stinking skunk!

NURSE: [*clutching the stole tightly*] For the sake of our poor mother! Please calm yourself!

[*The* PATIENT's *arms drop. She is overcome with grief. She stares into space. The* NURSE *disappears through the door.*]

PATIENT: [*with total abandon*] Mamma . . .

[*There is no response.*]

[*in the voice of a little girl*] I promise I'll behave, I'll go straight back to bed . . . [*She lies down on the bed.*] Dora's right . . . I was always highly strung . . . a girl must be gentle, otherwise nobody will love her, isn't that so? . . . She must be gentle, but not a fool . . . I passed all my exams, I was a model student . . . but it never crossed my mind that he was carrying on with another woman. You both knew and didn't let on. And you didn't say a word to spare me the blow. [*submissive, girlish*] You weren't looking for dirt, but somehow you always found it. What's the use now? The wife is always the last one to find out . . . I don't bear a grudge against either of you . . . because neither of you had as much as I did . . . Dora didn't go to college and my husband was always rolling in money . . . And now you're both gone and I'm still alive . . . I don't bear a grudge . . . I couldn't . . . or could I? . . . if I dared be mean . . .

[*She lays her head on the pillow and closes her eyes. The naturalistic light returns, and with it the* NURSE *appears at the door with her cap correctly placed, bearing a food tray.*]

NURSE: Señora . . . señora . . .

PATIENT: [*awakening*] What is it?

NURSE: Your supper.

PATIENT: [*resuming her usual intolerance and acidity*] Why are you bringing it? Where's the orderly?

145

NURSE: She knocked on the door but you were probably asleep.

PATIENT: Possibly...

NURSE: Rest is good for you. Did you have a pleasant dream?

PATIENT: I never dream. Or at least I'm never able to remember them if I do. Fortunately. [*cantankerous*] Stop gawping at my dinner! Anyone would think you were starved.

NURSE: It looks appetizing.

PATIENT: Where have you been all this time? ... Didn't you manage to have supper?

NURSE: I had a glass of milk.

PATIENT: You look positively undernourished. Put the tray down there. [*She indicates her bedside table.*]

NURSE: [*sweetly*] Very well, señora.

PATIENT: Aren't you ashamed to allow yourself to be treated this way? Or do you consider that my purse gives me the right to abuse you?

NURSE: [*carefully, thinking of what she is saying*] No one has the right to abuse anybody. Nevertheless, sometimes nerves make people lose their self-control so that they don't treat others properly, especially those closest to them.

PATIENT: People that "just grin and bear it" are idiots.

NURSE: One of the doctors I worked with somewhere else used to discuss this with us all the time because we were nursing people with nervous disorders.

PATIENT: You mean mental disorders. That hardly applies to me.

NURSE: [*A brief pause.*] This doctor would say that it was our duty to be forbearing because we had sound health and this gave us the resolve to cope with things. It was up to us to be strong because when others were temporarily ill, they

needed someone who was a little patient with
them. He'd say we shouldn't go home feeling
wretched because someone had walked all over
us that day . . .

PATIENT: [interrupting; intimately touched, not knowing
why] Walked all over. I haven't heard anyone
use that expression in years. Nowadays they say
"degrade" or "exploit," don't they?

NURSE: He'd say that once we've made the effort to be
patient, then it would be absurd to blame ourselves for having done so. You see, it would be
a contradiction.

PATIENT: Some advice.

NURSE: We do what we can. We can't always have
things our way. We're not God.

PATIENT: Things don't always come up trumps for Him
either.

NURSE: I don't agree.

PATIENT: Well, God's not going to get His way today. I
won't be offering you my dinner, for example.

NURSE: I don't know if I managed to explain it at all
well.

PATIENT: Oh, perfectly. Either you're very kind or very
scheming. [Brief pause.] Didn't you say you
wanted to eat my dinner so the doctor won't
throw you out on your ear?

NURSE: Yes, señora.

PATIENT: Then you needn't make the sacrifice. Just flush
it down the toilet instead.

NURSE: It's no sacrifice. I like the food. And I hate
wasting money in the canteen.

PATIENT: [fed up with people's problems, snorting] How can
you be so hard up if you've got a job and live
on your own?

NURSE: I had an unforeseen expense. But it's something
sad and I don't want to depress you.

147

PATIENT: Ha! I'll give you a medal if you manage to depress me any more than I am already.

NURSE: My mother was buried in a temporary plot. I've been postponing moving her, and now at the worst possible moment when it's so difficult to hold on to a job, I've had the final notice to have her remains transferred.

PATIENT: But what about your husband?

NURSE: I told you before—we're separated.

PATIENT: Yes ... but in the circumstances ...

[A noise is heard in the corridor.]

Please see what that is.

NURSE: [opening the door and peeking outside] Just a stretcher trolley.

PATIENT: Not from next door?

NURSE: [closing the door] No, they brought it out of the lift and went all the way down the corridor.

PATIENT: My last nurse was a real gossip. She told me everything that went on next door.

NURSE: Sometimes they leave the door open. I noticed there's a young woman in there.

PATIENT: But she's very ill. I've always been so competitive I challenged her. The one that dies first ... wins.

NURSE: NO! LOSES!

PATIENT: Wins! Who cares to live? God never gets things right in this world.

NURSE: You mean He does in the next.

PATIENT: Who knows? [serious] His luck might be even worse there. That's probably why I don't want to die.

NURSE: [to herself] Sometimes I do.

PATIENT: What did you say? I didn't get that.

NURSE: Nothing. It's a very delicate matter.

PATIENT: I don't feel like arguing. [Brief pause.] What is for dinner?

NURSE: Braised liver and mashed potatoes and apples in syrup.

PATIENT: Cut me a little of the liver—I want to give it a try. The first time I've ever tried a morsel of these crooks' food. The prices are outrageous here.

NURSE: [*trying to hide her pleasure, she picks up the cutlery*] In little pieces?

PATIENT: Just one slice. Put it on the side plate. You can have the rest.

NURSE: [*tries to hide her satisfaction.*] Very well. [*She cuts a slice of liver and serves it.*]

PATIENT: [*She retains the tray.*] So tell me—are you going to your grave livid with yourself because you never studied medicine?

NURSE: It looks that way. [*She sits to eat, holding the plate in one hand and the fork in the other.*]

PATIENT: You need qualifications to get into medical school, and you've not even got a school certificate. How old are you now?

NURSE: Forty-eight.

PATIENT: Get yourself off to night school and stop whimpering.

NURSE: With luck I might qualify in time for my sixtieth birthday.

PATIENT: [*eating*] Listen, if you're just out to gain pity, do nothing, carry on whingeing. But don't expect any pity from me—anyone who doesn't make the effort to pull themselves out of their hole deserves to stay there. It's not pity I feel for failures but ... something else.

NURSE: What?

PATIENT: Anger. Well, now I've eaten this rubbish. A little roll will take the awful taste away.

NURSE: You could have the apple in syrup.

PATIENT: Hospital food. You eat it! Give me the bread, I told you.

149

NURSE: [*offering the plate*] It's nice and fresh. The bread's always fresh here. You don't often find that in a hospital.

PATIENT: [*taking the roll*] You only know it's fresh because you've been squeezing it.
[*No reply.*]
Clean pig never gets fat, mamma used to say. [*She starts to eat.*]

NURSE: I never heard that saying before.

PATIENT: It may be fresh but it tastes like cardboard. I want to get rid of the taste of that liver. Look, give me a spoonful of that apple. Use this plate here. [*She passes the same plate to the* NURSE.]

NURSE: No, you take the bowl.

PATIENT: [*impatient, but now less acid*] A spoonful is what I said!
[*The* NURSE *looks at her and immediately serves her a spoonful.*]
[*trying to disguise her humour*] God can have the leftovers. Let Him give them to those whose need is greatest.
[*Black-out.*]

*I*nterlude music is heard. Daytime, after lunch. A couple of weeks later. Sitting on a sofa, in a housecoat, the PATIENT reads a newspaper. The NURSE arranges flowers in a vase. The telephone rings.

NURSE: Shall I answer it?

PATIENT: [*in high spirits*] Just . . . let it ring a little while.

NURSE: It's bound to be the doctor. No one else calls.

PATIENT: Precisely. Let's give him a scare. It infuriates me to pay him a fortune for doing nothing. Let me tease him a little, at least.

NURSE: [*laughing*] He'll just think they put him through to the wrong room and hang up.

PATIENT: [*Sharing the joke, she picks up the phone.*] Hello

... Ah, doctor! And how are you today? ...
[*grinning*] Me? Dreadful. So now you can stop
worrying. At least you know I can't get worse.
[*She gasps with a laugh.*] ... Why shouldn't I
laugh? Or do I need permission? Listen, I have
something to ask you. Now ... if one wanted
to become a doctor ... No, not me, of course,
I'm inquiring on behalf of my nurse ...
[*The* NURSE *signals that she doesn't want the matter discussed.*]
No, she doesn't have her school certificate ...
Over the last two weeks I've been able to drag
a few things out of her ... Further training to
specialize as a nurse? ... A scholarship? In
Spain? And when is the enrolment? ... Pity.
[*Pause.*] If people won't open their mouths, they
can hardly complain when they're overlooked
... Thank you, doctor ... No, [*abrupt*] we can
talk about me some other time. [*She hangs up
abruptly, giggling at her daring.*]

NURSE: [*fretting*] Now what'll he think of me?

PATIENT: Who cares? It gets you nowhere being so dif-
fident. As it turns out, he knew of a specialist
course that was taking place for nurses. Well,
psychiatric nurses to be precise.

NURSE: With a scholarship?

PATIENT: Yes, from the Spanish Embassy! One of those
exchange schemes. At a psychiatric institute.

NURSE: [*Uttering the almost sacred words, she holds her
hand to her bosom.*] The center in Bilbao ...

PATIENT: Yes, that's the one. How did you know about
it?

NURSE: They're always writing about it in the professional magazines. When I was working at the
other clinic, I used to take them home. But I'd
always return them, of course.

PATIENT: The doctor said he would have given you a good reference but he didn't know you were interested. He was on the selection panel.

NURSE: [*as if learning of a crime*] He was! Oh my God, how horrible! This could only happen to me.

PATIENT: Next time round, then!

NURSE: It's a wonderful place. They use the most up-to-date methods. There, they're not in it just for the money. They're genuine, selfless people.

PATIENT: There they kill you for free, here you have to pay.

NURSE: For them, nobody's totally sane, doctors and patients are on the same level, only the doctors want to know everything and the patients, in general, don't.

PATIENT: And you didn't know about the scholarship?

NURSE: [*with growing dismay at the chance she's lost*] No.

PATIENT: Something else will turn up.

NURSE: [*totally sceptical*] Not as good as this.

PATIENT: Something good has come of this already. We've discovered another avenue for your career. Why ask for the impossible, like going into medical school?

NURSE: [*bitterly*] The Bilbao institute. Someone's played a mean trick on me, it seems.

PATIENT: What nonsense is this? You never applied, they've never heard of you.

NURSE: [*pensive*] It's best to accept it. Better know your place and stop grumbling.

PATIENT: [*brightly*] Of course! There's only room for one grumbler in here, and that's going to be me . . . [*with humor*] but not now, time for that later. I think I'd rather have a nap if you'd draw the blinds.

NURSE: [*crossing to the blinds*] Right away, señora.

PATIENT: [*settling down*] It's a little like life, isn't it? A moment in the sun is nice, but then you long for the shade.

NURSE: Is that better?

PATIENT: Yes, thank you. Blessed relief. [*She closes her eyes.*]

[*The* NURSE *sits and lifts a hand to her brow, crestfallen, defeated. As the rest of the stage darkens, an unnatural light illuminates her.*]

NURSE: [sighs deeply] Ah! . . .

[*The* PATIENT *gets out of bed, but we note that her posture is now that of a woman who had endured a lifetime of service to others. She is an old woman weighed down by obedience and misfortune.*]

PATIENT: Will you want dinner tonight?

NURSE: [*without looking up: absorbed*] I don't know, señora. I'll just have whatever's left on your plate. But these last few days you haven't been leaving anything at all.

PATIENT: Don't call me "señora"! I'm your mother. All you have left in the world. Are you going to have something to eat or not?

NURSE: [*She hasn't looked at her yet.*] I don't know, mamma.

PATIENT: Today has been the hardest day of your life. We've just been to bury your poor father, and no sooner are we home than we feel weak with hunger. And there's not a thing ready.

NURSE: I'm not hungry.

[*A small kitchen table with a bag of potatoes, a knife and an apron comes out of the wardrobe. The* PATIENT *dons the apron, picks up the knife and begins peeling potatoes.*]

PATIENT: It's strange but one gets hungry anyhow. To tell the truth, I feel relieved. At least the poor man's out of his misery.

NURSE: [*She stands up and looks at the empty bed.*] Señora ... did you hear that? Mamma said I've got no one else but her in the world. It's not true, not really. But, of course, you won't want to hear all my problems with Miguel. He was my fiancé, we were engaged.

PATIENT: [*within the role of the mother until the end of the scene*] What you mean is you don't want to talk about him. This is a sad day, but not just for you! We've got to face things.

NURSE: [*She raises her head and looks at the* PATIENT *for the first time.*] Mamma ... I told Miguel not to come here any more. I told him I wouldn't see him again.

PATIENT: [*Visibly relieved by this news, she strokes the* NURSE's *head as if giving her absolution.*] I thought all along you knew what was right and you'd do it.

NURSE: Mamma. There's something I've been longing to ask you. Who told the story to papa?

PATIENT: Don't fret over your papa. The poor man's at peace at last.

NURSE: [*She quits the space now occupied by the mother, almost shouting.*] Señora! Don't pay any attention to what mamma says. There's not a word of truth in what she says. Papa didn't start going downhill just because he found out. He never liked Miguel. He always felt Miguel was too old for me.

PATIENT: I never liked him either. The way he used to gawp at us when we were eating, watching whether we used the right knife and fork. But at least we always had food enough. His family might have given him those airs and graces, but there was never anything to put on the end of his fork in that house.

NURSE: His family might have been stuck up, but he wasn't like that. He was different, more like us.

PATIENT: [*lightly sarcastic*] You saw his papers, didn't you? Fifty-seven if he was a day. If not older.

NURSE: Go ahead ... exaggerate as always. I saw his papers. I knew he was much older than me. But listen, mamma, a thirty-nine-year-old woman isn't exactly a slip of a girl.

PATIENT: Just tell me one thing. Did you get around to telling your papa you'd packed Miguel in?

NURSE: No. He was so ill it wouldn't have registered.

PATIENT: You were wrong there. He would have understood.

NURSE: How did ... how did papa find out?

PATIENT: I don't know. He wouldn't tell me ... his colleagues from the office came to see him. He was already in bed, but still at home, right before they took him into hospital.

NURSE: People warned me. But I thought it was all lies. [*Pause.*] I thought.

PATIENT: Your father got me to call Miguel one day while you were out at work. I asked him right out whether it was true his wife was still alive and hadn't passed away like he said. He broke into tears and admitted it was true. His wife was committed years ago.

NURSE: [*deeply disillusioned*] Why didn't he come out with it at the beginning? He must have known that sooner or later ...

PATIENT: He said he loved you and he was afraid of losing you.

NURSE: When he stopped coming to see papa, it was obvious what everyone was saying was true ... How shameful for papa.

PATIENT: It broke him. More even than his illness.

[*The* NURSE *repeats the earlier part of the scene*   155

with the same gestures and inflexion, neurotically.
She addresses the bed, seeking the absent patient.]

NURSE: Did you hear that, señora? There's not a word
of truth in what mamma says. Papa didn't start
going downhill just because he found out about
it all. He never liked Miguel. Papa always
thought he was too old for me.
[*The speed increases.*]

PATIENT: You saw his papers, didn't you? Fifty-seven at
least.

NURSE: Mamma. A thirty-nine-year-old woman isn't
exactly a slip of a girl.

PATIENT: Just tell me one thing. Did you get around to
telling your father you'd packed him in?

NURSE: No. He was so ill it wouldn't have registered.
[*She collapses into the chair and the* PATIENT
climbs slowly back into bed.] How did ... how
did papa find out? [*Silence.*] Mamma ... [*obedi-*
ently] I told Miguel not to come here anymore.
I'm not seeing him again.

PATIENT: I thought all along you knew what was right
and you'd do it.

NURSE: [*docilely*] Mamma ... [*Pause.*] Mamma ...
How? [*She loses her composure, stands and speaks*
with vehemence to the woman in the bed.]
Señora! Mamma isn't right! I didn't say anything to papa because he was already uncon-
scious by then, so what was the use?
[*Pause. The* PATIENT *has her eyes closed as before*
the hallucination.]
Señora! Why don't you answer me? Is it
because you've already seen through it? ... Perhaps you've already guessed that I knew the
whole story right from the beginning only I
didn't tell mamma ... [*with deep guilt*] ... I
knew all about Miguel! Only he never admitted

to it. I was hoping his wife would die ... What did she have to live for, anyway? ... Señora, you're not answering me ...

[*She flops into the chair while the light returns to the same level as before the hallucination.*]

PATIENT: [*recovering her normal identity, opens her eyes and sits up a little in bed*] Have you been dozing?

NURSE: [*returning to her normal self*] No.

PATIENT: You're run down ...

NURSE: [*standing up*] No, I was just thinking, that's all ... about problems with no solution.

PATIENT: It's this business with the scholarship, isn't it?

[*Noises come from the corridor.*]

What's going on? Just glance outside, will you? [*impatient*] What is it?

NURSE: [*having opened the door*] The patient next door. [*She closes the door behind her.*] They're discharging her.

PATIENT: But that sounded like a stretcher trolley.

NURSE: They're taking her in a wheelchair. She's got her outdoor clothes on.

PATIENT: That poor girl's got cancer. She's always to and fro, one day she's better, the next worse. Of course she doesn't know; it's better like that.

NURSE: But they should tell her. These days they always tell the patients everything.

PATIENT: Preposterous! If people have the bad taste to want to live—let them. Telling them the truth is the same as handing down a death sentence from, I don't know what, an unfair and whimsical tribunal. That illness *is* unfair and whimsical.

NURSE: But people should have the right to choose how to spend their last days.

PATIENT: Look ... [*annoyed*] You don't know what you're talking about. How can anyone under-

stand what it means to know ... time is running out? A person might be utterly wretched
or the worst criminal in the world, but if they
have time in front of them ... something could
just come along and everything might change.

NURSE: [*after a slight pause; deeply interested*] What is it
you would like to change?

PATIENT: Time isn't on my side.

NURSE: But if it were—what?
[*Pause.*]

PATIENT: Above all ... I should like to learn to treat
myself ... better.

NURSE: What makes you say that?
[*Pause.*]

PATIENT: My grandson, a comment he made to me one
day. He was very critical of us all, his mother,
me; he used to say we were all repressed, people
from another era. In his opinion, we treated
others badly because we treated ourselves
badly. He was only a young boy, of course, but
... so decent. But what else would you expect
a grandmother to say?

NURSE: Please. Go on, I'd like to hear more.

PATIENT: Now what made me remember that? He only
mentioned it once and I've never thought about
it since.

NURSE: What else did he say?

PATIENT: Just that. That we should try to be our own
best friend ...

NURSE: He said that ...

PATIENT: I suppose it must have been because he'd had
enough of seeing his family torturing each
other needlessly. He was tortured enough by
the rest of us, he used to say, so there was no
need for him to torture himself. And he was
grateful to us for the lesson!

[*The* NURSE *cannot restrain herself and kisses the* PATIENT *on the brow.*]
What's got into you?!

NURSE: Forgive me, I couldn't help myself.

PATIENT: That was Victor. He'd just give us a look and he saw us as we really were. He would have been a very special young man. But all it took was a stupid road accident, people racing out of town for the weekend on a Friday evening. God made a real mess of things that day, no one can tell me otherwise. I doubt He ever got anything right.

NURSE: [*after a short pause*] He did the day your grandson was born.

PATIENT: Yes, that's right ... that was a glorious day.
[*The* PATIENT *stretches out her hand for the* NURSE *to hold. The* NURSE *takes the hand in hers and the* PATIENT *smiles.*]
And from that day ... until the other, I ... walked on air. Twenty-two years of sheer happiness. What's your first name?

NURSE: Delia.

PATIENT: Delia ... You know, Delia, I've always had a weakness for the pastries from that German bakery just up the road. Victor used to adore them too; I had him quite hooked on them. Now, I wonder, would you mind awfully if I asked you to pop out and buy us a box? You like cakes, don't you?

NURSE: Mmm, yes, I have a sweet tooth too.

PATIENT: You don't mind going? Suddenly, I have a craving for a coconut slice. [*She opens her handbag on the night table and looks for the money.*] But get a good selection, will you. And we can keep them in the refrigerator. [*She gives the* NURSE *the money.*]

NURSE: I'll bring you back the change.

PATIENT: And open the blinds for me, will you?

[*The* NURSE *does so and light fills the room. The* PATIENT *now takes a ring from her handbag.*]

I'd forgotten all about my ring. Before, I never used to take it off.

NURSE: [*without noticing the ring*] I'll be back soon. Where is this place exactly?

PATIENT: Two streets away on Cabildo Avenue.

NURSE: [*leaving, full of spirits*] I'll be straight back.

[*The* PATIENT *slips on the ring and looks at it. Suddenly, a thought occurs to her and she picks up the telephone.*]

PATIENT: Hello ... How are you? ... Well, of course it's your mother. Did I scare you? ... There's no need to exaggerate. Of course I hadn't stopped speaking to you ... Myself, dreadful, but don't worry. I want you to do something for me. It's my nurse's pay day tomorrow ... I want to give her a raise. She hasn't had her due, the doctor only took her on with the utmost reluctance ... I beg your pardon? ... Her name's Delia, forty-eight years old, tall as a beanstalk ... You were there? ... Yes, it's the same one ... What do you mean, she took it as a favor to the doctor? ... What do you mean, she's in demand? The most sought after! Well, just how much are we paying her? ... He told me it was exactly half of that ... Why? ... Well, of course I would have objected ... Then you're quite sure they didn't take her on trial for two days? ... She took me on trial? [*trying not to show she has been deceived by all this*] What do you mean "as a favor"? ... For just three weeks? That means she's about served her time with me ... So why

does she have to go to a public hospital if she's
earning more privately? Union rules? ... I suppose because she doesn't have a diploma or
whatever ... She does? Are you positive? ...
So it's just to satisfy her union bureaucracy ...
And what about satisfying the needs of her
patients?!?! No, she hadn't fooled me, I could
smell something fishy as soon as I clapped eyes
on her ... Is it true that she's separated? ...
Not married. An old maid is what you mean.
No one ever pulls the wool over my eyes. And
what about her mother: is it true she passed
away? ... Last year? You may have been taken
in by that, but not me. You can't believe a word
people tell you. Don't be naïve. They're scum
... Of course not! Why on earth should I raise
her wages? ... Yes, indeed, pretend I never
said a word ... Yes, take care of yourself too
... bye-bye ... [*She hangs up.*]
[*Meanwhile the light in the room is changing as
night falls from red to violet.*]

NURSE: [*returning with the box of cakes*] I'm sorry it took
me such a long time.

PATIENT: [*enigmatic*] What happened?

NURSE: It was crowded and there was a queue.

PATIENT: [*cool*] Besides, it's some distance. Anyway, I've
lost my appetite now.

NURSE: Shan't I bother opening the box, then?

PATIENT: No ... [*She speaks in an ambiguous tone, part
playful, part threatening.*] But I have something
else that'll make your mouth water.

NURSE: [*taking part in what she thinks is going to be an
innocent tease*] Oh! What's that?

PATIENT: You'll forgive me if I appear to have been pre-
sumptuous, but you were so upset about that

scholarship that ... I made a little phone call while you were away. [*She now begins untying the box of cakes with great care.*]

NURSE: To who?

PATIENT: Guess.

NURSE: The doctor?

PATIENT: No ... Let's see ... think ... It was a call that changed everything ... [*maleficent*] for me. Ah! But what am I saying? It's your life that it could change.

NURSE: [*intrigued*] I can't imagine. I give up.

PATIENT: Very well, I'll tell you ... but give me your word you're not going to get all anxious.

NURSE: Ooh! ... I don't know ... Oh, all right then, I promise!

PATIENT: I have a friend at the Spanish Embassy, and he managed to put me in contact with the cultural attaché.

NURSE: [*truly excited*] Ooh, please, don't say any more ..

PATIENT: [*playfully*] Very well, I won't mention it again ...

NURSE: No. I'd best hear everything.

PATIENT: You can guess, I told him all about your case, and he said that he might consider further applications if the clinic in Bilbao is willing.

NURSE: Oh, but in that case ...

PATIENT: He's already sent the names, so he'll have to clear it with Bilbao ... but if they don't raise any objections, he has asked to interview you.

NURSE: It can't be true ... it's like a dream ...

PATIENT: It's a reality ... if you're prepared to fight for it.

NURSE: Señora ... How can I ever thank you?

PATIENT: You know, people can't fool me. I saw from the start you were someone full of secret ... longings.

NURSE: I forget about them, but you're right. I still have them. Buried deep down.

PATIENT: So dig them up. Don't always be the patient nurse. Do something wild. Isn't it your Bilbao people who say we're all a bit mad? Some who want to find out about things [*indicating the* NURSE] *and some who don't* [*indicating herself*].

NURSE: You learn quickly.

PATIENT: I wish I would. I never liked being the last one to find out about things. Listen. We shall need all our strength and resolve. Now that the box is open I feel like a cake again . . .

NURSE: I got the coconut slices.

PATIENT: Those you leave for me . . . [*She chooses one from the tray and eats it.*]

NURSE: Do you mind if I help myself?

PATIENT: [*making an effort to swallow, her mouth is full of cake*] Eat as many as you like . . . [*ironically*] It's your just dessert.

END OF ACT ONE

Act Two

Next day. The PATIENT, *a night-dress under her dressing-gown, reads a newspaper on the sofa. She displays considerably more vitality than hitherto. The* NURSE *sits on the bench and studies a nursing periodical.*

PATIENT: [*with a mere hint of irony*] Is it all coming flooding back now? Or had you forgotten everything?

NURSE: It must be my nerves, sometimes I get the feeling I've forgotten everything. I'm rereading the articles I collected about the Bilbao institute.

PATIENT: So you didn't give them all back when you left the clinic.

NURSE: There were a couple lying around at home.

PATIENT: [*spurred on by this revelation*] Hmm . . . You just carry on reading. I'm quite sure my lawyer will be able to put your nerves at rest.

NURSE: [*looking at her watch*] Are you positive he'll be able to see me today?

PATIENT: Of course. It's Wednesday, isn't it? And it's almost time for you to go and see him. That's what your nerves are all about.

NURSE: You're right. I'd better be going soon.

PATIENT: [*ironic*] There's no need to rush. He always keeps people waiting.

NURSE: Tell me what he's like.

PATIENT: Well . . . a nice man, really . . . considering what a shyster he is. On the whole, I think doctors are more attractive than lawyers, don't you?

NURSE: I didn't mean what does he look like. I meant is he good . . . understanding?

PATIENT: Obviously. [*sibylline*] I'm curious about your husband, you don't say much about him.

NURSE: He's dead.

PATIENT: Then you're a widow, not separated.

NURSE: I always tell people we're separated. But it isn't the truth. I just say that so as not to prolong the discussion. Actually, I was never married in the first place. We were together for a couple of years, but it all petered out. I'm still single.

PATIENT: But not an old maid.

NURSE: What's the difference?

PATIENT: Old maids are bitter, everyone knows that.

NURSE: Well, I'm bitter.

PATIENT: A tiny bit, perhaps. But old maids are riddled with regrets about the things they didn't do.

NURSE: So am I. Maybe I seized my chance. But what was it? A couple of hours once or twice a week in a hotel room. Some opportunity.

PATIENT: You are bitter, so that makes you an old maid. What a pity! [*with forced lightness*] ... But now things may change. [*treacherous*] My lawyer will give you a letter of recommendation the like of which you have never seen. When you take it along to the consulate, everything will go smoothly.

NURSE: [*grateful*] I wish I had your faith, señora.

PATIENT: That just shows that you don't think you deserve the scholarship. And, if that's the case, you needn't bother with the letter.

NURSE: No, please don't think that! I'm anxious because it means such a lot to me. It's like it's fallen from the skies. I didn't have to even talk to the cultural attaché. You and your lawyer have fixed it all up for me.

PATIENT: It's only a simple scholarship ...

NURSE: Don't you think I should have a word with him and fill him in on my details?

PATIENT: [*firmly*] No! You know what they're like, these diplomats, very pernickety. He gave me his word. Just deliver the letter to him at the consulate and let him get on with it.
[*Pause.*]

NURSE: I still can't believe it. It's like a dream coming true. I'd sooner die than lose it now.

PATIENT: Let's try to retain a sense of proportion.

NURSE: [*serious*] I am. It'll be the end of me if it all comes to nothing.

PATIENT: Now you're frightening me. [*with guarded humor*] What a thing to say ... Instead ... why don't you tell me what you're looking forward to in Bilbao? Tell me how you imagine what it'll be like.

NURSE: Oh yes ... I haven't been able to get it out of my mind.

PATIENT: Let your imagination run wild.

NURSE: That's just what they do in Bilbao.

PATIENT: The doctors or the lunatics? Ah, but I'm forgetting, they only have the one sort there.

NURSE: [*respectfully*] I'm serious. They chat like that a
lot, pure fantasy. And it's the doctors who start
the game.

PATIENT: Come on. Get on with it, close your eyes. Let's
go sightseeing.

NURSE: You promise you won't laugh at me?

PATIENT: You have my word.

[*Pause. The* NURSE *closes her eyes and throws her
head back.*]

NURSE: I'm on a ship, there's a lot of mist and I'm alone
on deck. I'm wearing a veil ... It's crazy, but
that's what I see.

PATIENT: Carry on.

NURSE: A man tells me he loves me. An interesting
man, with a secret. He is smoking a pipe and
has a beard.

PATIENT: But you'll be travelling by plane sitting next to
a woman with a screaming infant.

NURSE: One cold twilight, it's drizzling, I go back to
my cabin and I find a bouquet of roses. It will
be the first time that anyone has given me
flowers. But when I thank the man with the
beard, he replies that he didn't send them.

PATIENT: Who did?

NURSE: No one knows. The man wants me to run away
with him at the next port of call, but I don't
leave the ship. He does. The police arrest him.
There's been some misunderstanding. He
promises to come and look for me one day.

PATIENT: What's this man's secret?

NURSE: I don't know for sure ... but he isn't married,
not that ...

167

PATIENT: I think you're wrong. I'm sure he's married.

NURSE: [*firm*] No ... Anyway, I arrive in Bilbao and throw myself into my studies.

PATIENT: It rains a lot there in winter. I was there once.

NURSE: [*opening her eyes*] Really! What's it like? Do tell me!

PATIENT: No, you carry on, my own memories tire me. Continue ... spring is coming ...

NURSE: I'm standing in a garden, no, a patio, with lots of climbing plants ...

PATIENT: Jasmine.

NURSE: Yes. The smell is overpowering.

PATIENT: There is a man sitting, playing patience.

NURSE: People are watching, but it doesn't bother him.

PATIENT: No, he's alone although he'd like to have some company to play poker, but there's no one. He stares at a card.

NURSE: No, it's just that he's lost in his own thoughts. He doesn't notice my looking at him. And then he buries his face in his hands. Heartbroken.

PATIENT: Where is this patio? Is it in his house?

NURSE: No, I think it must be at the institute. I'm there on account of my scholarship.

PATIENT: Carry on, then.

NURSE: He's a relative of someone who's ill.

PATIENT: His son ...

NURSE: No, his wife, and he wants to take her back home with him. But I'm beginning to feel a little dizzy from this heady smell of jasmine, it's so sweet, and I tell him not to worry because I'm the nurse in charge of his wife, we'll soon go back to their house, all of us.

PATIENT: I know what's coming.

NURSE: Me too. The children are going to get attached to the nurse. And his wife too, of course. Only there's no hope for the unfortunate woman.

PATIENT: But there is hope for you?

NURSE: Perhaps. The scent of jasmine is inescapable; they even have jasmine in their gardens too.

PATIENT: What do you mean "gardens"? Sounds like a nursery.

NURSE: One summer's night, this is before his wife has passed away, I go for a walk. He's out there because he can't sleep either. And we succumb to temptation.

PATIENT: You talk like an old maid.

NURSE: That's what I am. Later the same night his wife rings for me. She's been feeling much worse and she asks me to promise to look after her children, and her husband too.

PATIENT: Answer me truthfully: do you want her to die?

NURSE: No!

PATIENT: [*amused, believing she's sensed the* NURSE's *lack of sincerity*] So you're hoping she's going to get better, then?

NURSE: The poor woman is terminal. If I thought there was any chance of her recovering, I wouldn't even look at her husband.

PATIENT: [*amused*] Needless to say. Shall we go on? . . . That very night, or only a couple of days later, the woman dies. [*ironic*] Let's say within a week so as not to keep you waiting.

NURSE: Later on we get married, we are happy.

PATIENT: What do you mean "happy"?

NURSE: Just that. Happy.

PATIENT: How do you spend your days? Cooped up in the house?

NURSE: No, I spend a lot of time in the gardens.

PATIENT: [*ironic*] But of course, you have more than one.

NURSE: But there are no roses. Until one day a bouquet **169** of them arrives for me and I put them in a vase believing he sent them to me. The same roses as on the ship.

PATIENT: You mean you're just married and you're already thinking of somebody else!

NURSE: He comes home and asks me who sent them.

PATIENT: Who did?

NURSE: No one knows, and then one day I realize I'm about to start a family of my own. [*She takes off her cap, her grey hair falls down.*]

PATIENT: At your age!

NURSE: You're right, I'd forgotten abut that. The thing is, in this dream, I'm only a young woman, no more than twenty-five or so. And that very day I write you a letter with the news.

PATIENT: Ah! I'd somehow thought of myself as well beneath the sod by then.

NURSE: You'll see us all in our graves.

PATIENT: What makes you say that?

NURSE: You're strong, that's why.

PATIENT: You're not pretending ... really, I don't come to a sudden end in this tale of yours?

NURSE: No.

PATIENT: [*canny*] You do away with the wife, but I'm spared ...

NURSE: That's the way it seems, apparently ... when I close my eyes and imagine.

PATIENT: Please, do go on. After you've had the baby, do you go back to work at the institute, do you keep up your studies?
[*Pause.*]

NURSE: No, I stay at home to look after my own children and the children from the first marriage. And we all live happily.

PATIENT: [*suddenly losing all her sense of humour*] No!

Don't do it, I beg you! He'll come home like a bear with a sore head every night!

NURSE: No, he won't. But there is something that worries me. You see, I didn't have much of an education, and I'm ashamed to admit that I don't know how to hold the cutlery properly.

PATIENT: That is completely ridiculous. You're making a great mistake giving up your career. Don't let yourself stagnate staying at home!

NURSE: No, if he brings problems home from the office, he's going to find a sympathetic ear . . .

PATIENT: [*agitated*] No! Please! You're making a huge mistake!

[*The* NURSE, *now worried herself by the* PATIENT's *frenzy, crosses and holds the* PATIENT's *hand in hers.*]

NURSE: What is it, señora? Are you feeling poorly?

PATIENT: Yes . . . [*She gets back into bed.*] Pay no attention to me . . . Please sit down and continue with your story.

NURSE: Are you sure?

PATIENT: [*serious*] I'm asking you to.

NURSE: [*She sits down.*] All right . . . [*closes her eyes*] Where were we?

PATIENT: You were writing me a letter.

NURSE: Yes, and it went unanswered. You never answered any of my letters. That was the only cloud. Otherwise, the sky was sunny and clear.

PATIENT: Oh . . .

NURSE: Well, then, I think I should be getting along to this appointment, don't you?

PATIENT: Yes . . . Tell me: you're not going to get upset because I didn't answer your letters, are you?

NURSE: Naturally it saddens me. I don't get any other letters from home because I have no family there anymore. But you can't have everything, I suppose, can you?

PATIENT: It wouldn't matter, would it? We were just playing a game . . .

NURSE: Yes, but it's late . . .

PATIENT: You've got the address and everything, haven't you?

NURSE: Yes. I'll be back as soon as I can.

PATIENT: Try to stay calm.

NURSE: [*leaving*] See you later.

PATIENT: Bye-bye. [*As soon as she hears the* NURSE *walking away, she grabs her address book and dials a number.*] Hello . . . Put me through to Gomez Viaggio's secretary, please . . . Ah, you recognized my voice . . . Yes, still unwell, thank you . . . [*trying to avoid small talk*] not quite better . . . So let's not waste time chatting. Tell me, my lawyer isn't there, is he? . . . No, I know he doesn't come to the office on Wednesdays, I just thought there might be some reason why he'd be there today . . . No, that was all. I just wanted to make sure he wasn't there. Listen, my nurse is going to drop by, tell her that he's had to step out unexpectedly, would you? But don't mention the fact that he's never there anyway on a Wednesday. Will you do me this favor? I'm so grateful. Goodbye.
[*She hangs up, starts to feel anxious and buries her head in the pillow.*]

There is a very sudden change in atmosphere, the lights go out, the door is pushed open and the NURSE *enters angrily. She has her cap back on, her walk and her speech are completely different, she acts like a determined and temperamental woman.*

NURSE: Mother! How could you so such a thing to me!! Why didn't you give evidence???

PATIENT: [*half asleep*] What is it? What are you doing here?

NURSE: Don't pretend! Wake up! Aunt Dora is furious with you. Why didn't you warn anyone you wouldn't testify on my behalf? Oh, no, you had to go behind my back, didn't you? I hear it's the best position to put the knife in.

PATIENT: I hardly recognize you with that nurse's hat on. Why don't you pick yourself something of your own from the closet over there? That cap *doesn't* belong to you.

NURSE: Mother ... you're so grey! Everyone dyes their hair these days, so why do you have to make yourself look like a blessed saint with those white locks?

PATIENT: [*getting out of bed*] What did the lawyer say?

NURSE: [*exasperated, reproachful*] What would you expect him to say? It's going to be a catastrophe! That's what! Cesar has undeniable proof of adultery. And you wouldn't even raise a finger to help me by testifying against him.
[*The* PATIENT *finds a black hat and puts it on the* NURSE.]

PATIENT: This hat is very becoming yet quite sober at the same time. It was a wise move wearing something like that.

NURSE: Appearances count in court. I tried to make the best impression I could, although, personally, I loathe that sort of hypocrisy.

PATIENT: [*She takes a handbag from the wardrobe.*] You didn't smoke, did you?

NURSE: Of course not! Although I had my handbag beside me throughout. [*She opens the bag.*] I'll have one now, though. [*She lights a cigarette.*]

PATIENT: He's left the house, he's sleeping somewhere else, where will he take little Victor, then?

173

NURSE: He's only after custody. Once he's got that, he'll hand the boy over to one of us to look after for him. All he wants is the control.

PATIENT: Victor would be better off with me. That way he needn't see this man you're carrying on with.

NURSE: Mother! I've never brought him to the house! At least, never during the day when the child's around.

PATIENT: [*caustic*] I don't know how you have the gall to get up to the things you do!

NURSE: Mother ... [*She takes her hand, making an effort to communicate.*] you must try to understand that not everyone has your gift for self-control. Some people are different, they can't all live according to your lights. I felt I was drowning: I couldn't bear to see my life being whittled away and nothing to show for it. I'm not built like you. I'm more like father.

PATIENT: He wasn't like that.

NURSE: Mother, you're not being fair. The way you talk, anyone would think the world is over-flowing with saints and I'm the only one who's ever in the wrong.

PATIENT: But it is wrong to throw away your home just because some man appears on the scene. You may like him, but I don't believe you're deeply in love. You were terribly irresponsible, that's what I think.

NURSE: But one must have something to cling to ... some illusion.

PATIENT: Your child should be your great illusion. Your problem is you just can't shoulder responsibility, you're immature.

NURSE: It wasn't illusion enough for father either. You know what he was like.

PATIENT: I don't know why you're raking over that again. Your father was foolish just the once, but he wouldn't let it break up the family. Whoever's been telling you about all that has no right to. It was just the one time.

NURSE: Oh, mother, let's not talk about it anymore. Everyone—and you better than most—knew he was incapable of saying no.

PATIENT: Everybody knew about that one woman because I made a scandal over it. But there was never anyone else. Or do you think I'm totally stupid!?!?!

NURSE: He was notorious for the way he carried on. He just couldn't keep his hands to himself. Any woman would do ... Why only today Aunt Dora was telling me how he couldn't even keep his hands off her, his own sister-in-law—and her husband not two feet away! He had wandering hands.

PATIENT: Did she really say that?

NURSE: Yes—hardly an earth-shattering revelation.

PATIENT: Your father ... was always fond of a joke. He was playful. [*She becomes withdrawn.*]

NURSE: [*realizing that she has wounded her mother*] Mother ... What's upset you now?

PATIENT: I've never had the stomach for slander—it revolts me.

NURSE: I'm sorry, mother. Please forgive me. But it gets you nowhere burying your head in the sand, either. We women have been doing that for too long, and it never did us any good. I'm not going to take it up at my age. It's not my fault if that's the way he was.

PATIENT: [*making an effort to face the truth*] But is that ... is that what people think of him?

NURSE: [*understanding that perhaps this is the first time*] *her mother has acknowledged the truth*] Well now ... perhaps ... I suppose so ...

PATIENT: [*looking into her eyes*] I never ... knew.

NURSE: Knew what, mother?

PATIENT: That everyone knew ... but me. They say the wife is always the last to find out.

NURSE: [*repentant*] But ... you don't have to believe everything you hear ... it might just be silly gossip. [*Very worried, she moves closer to her mother to touch her, but it is obvious that she is unused to expressing her feelings.*] And no one ever breathed a word to you?

PATIENT: [*rejecting the gesture*] In any case ... I didn't register it if they did. [*curt*] Now, please leave me alone.

NURSE: No ... now that we've started to talk things over, mother, we ought to finish.

PATIENT: I'm awfully tired ... [*She gets back in the bed.*] I'd like to be left alone to rest.

NURSE: Whatever you like, mother.

[*The daughter draws closer to tuck the mother in bed: the mother lifts off the hat from the daughter's head.*]

PATIENT: Take this off, you're not in court now. I may be ill but I don't need you fussing over me. The nurse is here to look after me. She's just like you, she wears a hat to work the same way you did to go to court. But nobody's taken in by the costume, let me tell you. You're both charlatans! Now get out of here please!

NURSE: Very well ... But don't blame me if I turned out like father ... [*She leaves.*]

PATIENT: Phoneys! Hypocrites, the pair of them! All women are liars, I thank God my grandchild is a boy ... He's the only one of them all that matters to me ... But he's always got his nose in a book, he doesn't have time anymore to come and see his grandmother. I can't even ring him up, he gets irritated if I interrupt him while he's working ... Maybe I'll give him a call later, around dinner time ... But I'll find the number now. [*She leans over to find her address book on the bedside table.*] I never used to have to look it up. Is my memory going? [*She looks for the book.*] Victor ... Victor ... This is my new address book, I wrote everything down myself ... Why isn't Victor's name down here? [*She puts the book back on the table.*] I'll call later, I don't feel so good just now ... oh ... oh ... someone ... please ... someone please come and help me ... [*She rings the bell for the* NURSE.]

[*Loud disturbing ringings and sounds and turbulent lighting effects.*]

A yellow afternoon light filters through the blinds. The PATIENT *is sleeping. The* NURSE *stands with her arms folded, looking into the street, thinking.*

PATIENT: [*coming round*] Please ... what's the time?

NURSE: It's four P.M.

PATIENT: I don't understand ...

NURSE: [*She crosses and takes the* PATIENT's *pulse.*] How are you feeling today?

PATIENT: I can't open my eyes properly ... Have I been asleep long?

NURSE: The doctor came to see you yesterday morning and he gave you a sedative. When I was out.

PATIENT: I don't understand ...

NURSE: Don't you remember? Your blood pressure shot up and you weren't feeling too bright.

PATIENT: [*annoyed*] But didn't I warn you never to let that happen. I don't want sedatives!

NURSE: But I wasn't here, señora. You sent me to see your lawyer.

PATIENT: Wasn't that this morning?

NURSE: No, Wednesday, yesterday. And then the doctor gave you another sedative last night at bedtime.

PATIENT: What happened ... at the lawyer's?

NURSE: [*innocently*] He wasn't there. You must have muddled up the days.

PATIENT: [*ironic*] Oh, what a pity ...

NURSE: Anyhow, I can't tell the doctor what to do or not to do. Even if I had been here.

PATIENT: [*with a touch of sadism, wounding*] You weren't here when I needed you most.

NURSE: [*innocently*] That's what I thought, such bad luck. I didn't even want to go either.

PATIENT: But you did. Where's my hanky?

NURSE: [*trying not to answer offhandedly*] It's just that you told me to go in the first place ... [*She points to the drawer of the bedside table.*]

PATIENT: [*opening the drawer and taking out her handkerchief*] Where are my barbiturates? Where have they got to?

NURSE: The doctor told me to remove them. You might have woken up during the night and taken one without knowing you'd already been given a powerful sedative.

PATIENT: Where are they?

NURSE: In the cupboard.

PATIENT: What else did the doctor tell you?

NURSE: He seemed quite worried. Your blood pressure had gone up. But once he gave you the sedative, it returned to normal. He was giving you the injection himself, I got back just then.

PATIENT: What else?

NURSE: Then he came back in the evening. He called around midday to talk to me.

PATIENT: To you?

NURSE: Yes, to ask about you naturally.

PATIENT: And that's all you spoke about?

NURSE: [*trying hard not to broach the subject*] Er, yes. I raised something or other about the scholarship.

PATIENT: [*Irritated, she jumps as if prodded with a pin.*] You shouldn't have done that.

NURSE: I thought he knew all about it. I was so on edge after the mix up at your lawyer's office. And then when I got back here, you were ill. I know I shouldn't have said anything, but it's just that everything was conspiring to ...

PATIENT: [*interrupting*] Obviously, it would all come to a sudden end if I died.

NURSE: I didn't mean it to sound like that ...

PATIENT: No, don't apologize, I'm not upset by that, it's ... [*inventing*] it's, well, to be blunt, the reason is that the doctor doesn't like you.

NURSE: [*believing her every word*] I had no idea ...

PATIENT: Well, now that you've put your spoke in, you may as well tell me the damage.

NURSE: There's not much to tell. I had to explain about the cultural attaché, of course, how you'd managed to persuade him to consider my application. And I thought the doctor knew all about it.

PATIENT: [*inventing*] I hadn't wanted to involve him because I knew he'd try and block me. My plan was to present him with a *fait accompli*. Anyhow, did he say anything else?

NURSE: He said exactly the opposite. He told me to get in touch with the consulate and ask the cultural attaché to call him as soon as everything is ready.

PATIENT: [*tense*] You haven't called yet, have you?

NURSE: No. I thought it best to leave it to you once you were feeling better.

PATIENT: [*craftily*] Thank goodness for that ... But you shouldn't have said a word to him. What a foolish mistake! I shall do my best to put us back on the rails ... [*sadistically*] rather than under them.

NURSE: It was clumsy ... you're right.

PATIENT: I think it would be a good move to call the doctor right now. I've already sung your praises to him, but a little more can't do any harm.

NURSE: Are you sure you've got the strength?

PATIENT: No, but it will be easier if you're not standing there looking at me. Why don't you take a stroll around the corner, fill your lungs with fresh air ...

NURSE: Now?

PATIENT: Well, of course, now! What're you waiting for?

NURSE: [*Not convinced she's doing the right thing, she leaves.*] I'll be right back.

[*The* PATIENT *straightens up with difficulty, gets out of bed and picks up the* NURSE's *handbag, takes off her diamond ring and buries it in the bottom of the handbag, climbs back into bed and dials a number.*]

PATIENT: Put me through to the porter's office, please ... This is the patient in Room 217. I have a rather delicate request to make ... My nurse, I mean my own private nurse, is just on her way out ... You know her! So much the better because I want you to have a look inside her handbag when she leaves work today ... Oh, just a few things, of course I can't believe it could be her, but you never can tell . . . But since she isn't one of the regular staff, it shouldn't be too difficult to bend the rule and have a look inside her handbag, should it? And do call me right away, won't you? . . . That is, of course, if she's the thief . . . Thank you so much. I shall make it worth your while. . . . You're welcome. [*She hangs up. She is now on edge herself. She gets up. There is a knock at the door.*]

NURSE: [*enters*] Did you call him?

PATIENT: Yes . . .

NURSE: Shall I ring for a pot of tea?

PATIENT: Wouldn't you like to hear how it went first?

NURSE: My priority is to look after you, señora.

PATIENT: I'm truly sorry. It's bad news. He won't have any of it. In particular, he says it's because of your age. He says you're too mature.

NURSE: [*unable to contain herself*] It's so unfair.

PATIENT: I objected in the strongest terms. But then he had something else up his sleeve. He said you didn't have the right qualifications. He said that you'd be—as it were—an emissary of the country and your qualifications didn't come up to scratch.

NURSE: Oh . . . [*Silence.*] What is it about me that he objects to?

PATIENT: I simply think he has a different category of person in mind.

NURSE: Don't worry about offending me, señora. Be honest with me. It's best to hear the truth.

PATIENT: The truth hurts.

NURSE: I don't mind.

PATIENT: Well, I'm afraid he thinks you don't have the correct . . . background. He mentioned that he'd seen you eating, for instance, and that your manners . . . left a lot to be desired. You didn't hold your cutlery properly.

[*The* NURSE *remains immobile, as if a stone statue. Silence.*]

I think it's something of an exaggeration, unfair even . . . as you said yourself.

[*The* NURSE *still doesn't respond.*]

Do you understand what I'm saying?

[*There is a sudden brisk light change. What happens hereafter takes place in the* NURSE's *own mind. The* PATIENT *speaks in the voice of the* NURSE's *mother. She flops back on to the bed as if extremely ill.*]

What's wrong with you? Why won't you speak? . . . Well, why should I be surprised, we never understood each other much, did we? But we don't have much time left now . . .

NURSE: Don't say that, mamma. The doctor thinks you're a little better.

PATIENT: Delia . . . Do you mind if I bring up something sad?

NURSE: No, mamma, let's not talk about sad things . . .

PATIENT: I must, Delia. I have to tell you something, it has to be now. I may die at any moment.

NURSE: [*weary of hearing something which is true but not wanting to acknowledge it in front of her sick mother*] Of course you're getting better . . . [*without conviction*] You shouldn't talk like that.

PATIENT: I want to ask you to forgive me.

NURSE: Please, mamma . . . let's not talk like this. Leave it for another day when you're up and about.

PATIENT: No, really, it can't wait . . . Listen to me, I want you to forgive me. I did you a terrible wrong.

Miguel wasn't a bad man, and I had no right
to be so . . . demanding . . . and hard.

NURSE: Mamma, I don't want to talk about all this.

PATIENT: I've been thinking. When I go, you'll be all
alone. I can't ask Miguel to forgive me, God
rest him, but I can ask you . . .

NURSE: Poor Miguel . . . it's been so many years since
he died. You know something, mamma? [*She
almost smiles.*] I think about him more since he
died than I did when he was alive. When we
stopped seeing one another . . . I did everything
I could to forget about him. And, honestly, I
didn't think of him after that until I heard that
he died.

PATIENT: It would have been easier if you'd seen him
when he became ill. It's awful when someone
dies . . . and there's no chance to say goodbye.
Listen, Delia, this is my goodbye to you . . .

NURSE: Don't talk that way, mamma.

PATIENT: No, this weakness seems . . . every day it . . .

NURSE: [*interrupting*] Don't strain yourself, mamma,
don't talk . . .

PATIENT: [*using all her strength*] You didn't answer me . . .
Can you forgive me? Or not?

NURSE: I forgive you, mamma, yes [*her voice strangled
with feeling*] . . . but the truth is . . . there's nothing to forgive . . . you were right . . . he
behaved badly.

PATIENT: No, no, he didn't . . . Miguel only deceived us
because he was so frightened he would lose you
. . . He was already a middle-aged man and
he'd had his share of suffering . . . first that
invalid wife of his, and he couldn't stand losing
everything a second time . . . you were all that
mattered to him . . . And it's true that he loved

you so much ... it was sadness that made him ill ... sadness kills us all eventually ... it's the start of every sickness. But you can rest assured that he loved you with all his heart.

NURSE: Thank you, mamma ... don't torture yourself about it.

PATIENT: Does that mean you've forgiven me?

NURSE: [*letting her go and resuming her position as before this hallucination*] Yes, mamma ...

PATIENT: Where are you going? Don't let my hand go ...

NURSE: [*talking to herself*] Your hand is cold, mamma. Frozen. And I need someone to help me ... I'm the one who needs help, and there's nothing you can do for me now you're dying. And here I am asking you to help me! You were never able to help me with the slightest thing ... So why am I asking you now? ... Perhaps because you brought me into the world ... and I have to thank you for that. No one else ever did anything for me, I don't owe anyone any favors ... only you for having brought me into this world where God never gets things right.

PATIENT: [*with the last grains of her strength*] Are you sure no one else ever helped you?

NURSE: Yes, that's true, there was someone, a crazy old woman who tried to put me forward for a scholarship.

PATIENT: Old like me?

NURSE: Yes, she's lucky too, like you, because she's also on the verge of dying. How I envy the pair of you! You're almost through, but I have to go on breathing the stench in this sewer!

PATIENT: You don't mean it.

NURSE: I do, this sewer. You brought me into this world. And it's a sewer. And I should be grateful for that. Well, I'm not, all I want is that you die now, soon, like that other one. Yes, Miguel's wife, shut away in a hospital for years and years, and she wouldn't die and me wishing minute by minute she would. And I wish you would too. The pair of you. Now.

[*Pause.*]

Do you see what you brought into this world, a bitter old maid who wishes everyone who crosses her path dead ... a path that leads nowhere ...

[*The natural light comes back on, the* PATIENT *becomes her usual self again, and finds herself at the exact moment when the break with reality took place.*]

PATIENT: Don't you understand what I'm saying? Why are you looking at me like that?

NURSE: [*suddenly calm, accepting utter defeat*] Nothing, señora ... I was just thinking ... I ought to tell you you're the only person who's ever tried to help me.

PATIENT: What are you talking about?

NURSE: It's true, you tried to help me, you discovered all about that absurd scholarship ... absurd only because I never have any luck. And that seemed like a fabulous stroke of luck. How stupid I was to think anything could ever come of it! But you did have the idea in the first place. It's not your fault if I don't deserve it.

PATIENT: [*unexpectedly telling the truth*] Yes, that's true, there was a moment when I wanted to help ...

NURSE: Señora ... I won't be able to come tomorrow. Will it be a great inconvenience to find a substitute?

PATIENT: Just for the day?

NURSE: No, I think you should look for someone on a more permanent basis.

PATIENT: I don't understand.

NURSE: Let me be candid, señora. What you really need is someone cheerful, who can lift your spirits. Otherwise, you're fine . . .

PATIENT: Fine . . . ?

NURSE: [*simultaneously kind and firm*] Yes, medically you're right as rain. Your blood pressure, blood sugar, liver, everything's fine. You are sick with sadness and I don't know how to cure that. I can't help you. I don't feel competent to do that.

PATIENT: You don't . . .

NURSE: I can fix up a substitute nurse tomorrow.

PATIENT: [*perplexed, uselessly trying to understand what's going on*] I could have one of the clinic's nurses in the meantime . . .

NURSE: In that case I can start to rest from tomorrow. Tonight I'll begin my rest. Starting tonight.

PATIENT: The bad news really did you in . . .

NURSE: No . . . it wasn't bad news . . . just a confirmation of what is my proper place.

PATIENT: You look worn out, aren't you feeling very well?

NURSE: Worn out, yes. That's the word. Would you mind if I left now?

PATIENT: Whatever you like . . .

NURSE: Really . . . I'm absolutely drained today. But there's something I'd like to say.

PATIENT: What's that?

NURSE: Do you mind if I pull up this chair to the bed? My legs won't hold me anymore.

PATIENT: [*very curious*] Please . . .

NURSE: [*She just leans on the chair, doesn't sit down.*] You feel very unhappy. With cause, because you suffered a terrible misfortune. But maybe you're forgetting there were other days when God got

His way, like the day when your grandson was born. God got it right that day, didn't he? And wasn't it Victor who told you so himself?

PATIENT: Told me what?

NURSE: That you had to be a good friend to yourself.

PATIENT: Indeed he did.

NURSE: And that's why I want to ask you something: you mentioned that your husband was a bit of a ladies' man . . .

PATIENT: Quite a lot of a ladies' man . . .

NURSE: But you never told me how he died.

PATIENT: It happened at home. He'd been ill a long time. He was a heavy smoker and it went to his lungs.

NURSE: And you always stood by him?

PATIENT: Always. During the last two years of his life, when he really felt bad, he never went out. Those friends he couldn't live without and their poker games . . . it all came to an end. I learned how to play to keep him company.

NURSE: Then he chose you to be at his side when his end came?

PATIENT: Yes, that's the way it happened.

NURSE: That's all I wanted to know, just that.

PATIENT: [*deeply affected by what she has only now understood*] I never looked at it like that.

NURSE: I'll be going, then.

PATIENT: Just a minute . . . I've a little favor to ask. Would you mind stepping out into the corridor for a moment?

NURSE: I'm just on my way out anyway. Shall I call the duty nurse?

PATIENT: No, please, just for a minute, a few seconds . . . Oh, please, you've put up with so many of my whims, this is the last one, I beg you . . .

NURSE: [*taking her handbag*] Two minutes . . .

PATIENT: No, leave your handbag, otherwise you'll forget to come back . . .

NURSE: [*Without understanding what's going on, she leaves the handbag.*] All right. [*She leaves.*]
[*The* PATIENT *gets up and removes the diamond ring from the handbag. She picks up the telephone and dials a number.*]

PATIENT: Porter's office, please . . . Engaged? Well, can't you interrupt the call? This is an emergency . . . It makes no difference what sort of emergency . . . [*highly agitated*] No, no, please insist, this is a real emergency . . . [*The* PATIENT *is deeply moved by the* NURSE's *explanation. She looks at the ring, and puts it on her finger.*]

NURSE: [*enters*] All done?

PATIENT: [*forced to hang up the telephone*] Yes, thank you . . . But I want to ask . . . do you think that that choice is important? . . . I mean the person someone chooses to have beside them when the end comes . . .

NURSE: It's the person one cherishes most in the world, isn't it?

PATIENT: Victor had just turned eight at the time, but my husband called him to his bedside and asked him to look after me as long as I lived . . . [*Pause.*] Thank you . . . I don't want to keep you any longer . . . If you ever have a spare moment, please telephone me some day.

NURSE: [*without conviction*] Yes . . . [*She goes to the wardrobe.*] I don't think I've left anything behind, have I? [*She opens the door and furtively puts something in her pocket.*] Ah, there it is . . . my time sheet . . . I always left it there . . .

PATIENT: I never noticed it . . .

NURSE: I don't like farewells . . . Good luck, señora . . .

[*She kisses her quickly.*] Thank you for everything ... I'm sorry I never had the chance to meet your grandson, he must have been a fine boy ... [*She leaves quickly.*]

[*The PATIENT is alone onstage. She takes a few steps. Inexplicably, she feels improved. She breathes with less difficulty. She takes a deep breath and opens the window and looks out into the receding distance.*]

PATIENT: Victor ... Victor ... somehow I know you're close ... please don't go away anymore ... Victor, you were given the responsibility to look after me, you won't forget that, will you? ... And don't forget who told you that, it was a man I loved a great deal ... always. [*The telephone rings. The PATIENT at first hesitates and then relents.*] Hello ... Porter? Oh, yes, I wanted to speak ... What's the matter? ... My nurse? ... What? ... In her handbag? ... Are you quite sure? ... Please have her come to my room immediately ... [*She hangs up. She stands upright, prepared to do battle.*]

NURSE: [*She comes in, her head lowered. Pauses.*] May I come in?

PATIENT: [*reaching out*] Give them back to me ...

NURSE: [*She takes two pill bottles from her handbag.*] I'm sorry ...

PATIENT: Two bottles of barbiturates. What did you intend doing with them, may I ask?

NURSE: [*her head still bent downwards*] Rest. Once and for all.

PATIENT: [*Pause. She indicates upwards.*] It appears someone had other ideas ...

NURSE: [*dry*] I never had much faith in Providence.

PATIENT: Then have faith in porters.

NURSE: Please let me go now ...

PATIENT: No. If you leave I shall report you for theft. If you stay ... I promise ... I don't know, something different.

NURSE: [*exhausted*] Señora, I'm sorry, but I'm in no mood for games.

PATIENT: This time it isn't a game. [*An idea occurs to her.*] Let's do something fantastic! ... Let's take a trip, to Spain, to Bilbao. Scholarship or no scholarship, we'll go to Bilbao, I could do with the change of air, and you could do with ... a project.

NURSE: I don't have the strength anymore.

PATIENT: If I do, then you shall too. Everything's turning out right today, don't you think? The porter has never searched your handbag before, has he? [*She puts her arm around the* NURSE's *neck. Her first display of feeling.*]

NURSE: You're right, it's very peculiar, no one has ever looked in my bag before ...

PATIENT: There's nothing peculiar about it at all! Sometimes God gets it right ...

NURSE: It certainly looks that way. [*She kisses the* PATIENT *on the cheek.*] Thank you.

PATIENT: [*crying with happiness*] Although, personally, I think that today ... the devil had a hand in it.

NURSE: No, let's just say it was the porter who helped.

PATIENT: As you like, dear. I have a sudden craving for something sweet, cakes ...

NURSE: Really? Would you like me to go and fetch some of the ones you like so much?

PATIENT: No, it's too far. Let's just have something from here. As long as it comes with lashings of sugar.

NURSE: [*contented; pauses*] A question. What's the correct way to eat a pastry? With a spoon or with a dessert fork?

PATIENT: Well, it's really rather complicated, you see. If

it's a puff pastry, then definitely with a fork. But a rum baba, on the other hand, is best eaten with a spoon.

NURSE: There's so much I have to learn.

PATIENT: [*with humor*] Quite. [*A sudden flash of inspiration.*] I know ... It's a beautiful summer evening, scorching hot, and the dinner table has been laid out on the patio...

NURSE: Beneath the jasmine. And someone arrives unexpectedly.

PATIENT: Don't tell me it's the same man who was on the boat.

NURSE: Yes, and he's telling the two of us so many stories about all the things that have happened ...

PATIENT: We carry on listening until it grows dark.

NURSE: He doesn't want to go, he's so enchanted with us. Time goes by like in a dream.

PATIENT: And then a storm breaks and he has to spend the night.

NURSE: There's thunder and lightning and outside it's pouring with rain. But inside there's a fire crackling in the hearth.

PATIENT: I open the lace curtains in order to see the storm in all its splendor, but it's almost time for me to retire and rest. I want to be alone to remember the many times I received a rose bouquet.

NURSE: Were they many?

PATIENT: [*with satisfaction and interior light*] Yes, I had forgotten.

NURSE: Suddenly, he remembers that he must go back to where he's come from. He has given his solemn promise. Duty calls him. He has to go. He's gone.

PATIENT: You're heartbroken, but in fact it is the greatest night of your life: Tonight you have to decide

191

your destiny. [*with humor*] To serve science, or love. Will it be the bustling activity of the hospital ward or the waiting in a garden, languishing, sunset after sunset ... [*Pause.*] Making yourself dizzy with the scent of jasmine.
[*They both laugh contentedly.*]

CURTAIN